BERLITZ®

FREN
WEST INDIES

1989/1990 Edition

By the staff of Berlitz Guides

Printed in Switzerland by Weber S.A., Bienne.

7th Printing
1989/1990 Edition

Updated or revised in 1989, 1988, 1984, 1982

How to use our guide

- All the practical information, hints and tips that you will need before and during the trip start on page 102.

- For general background, see the sections The Islands and the People, p. 6, and A Brief History, p. 13.

- All the sights to see are listed between pages 25 and 72. Our ![symbol] own choice of sights most highly recommended is pin-pointed by the Berlitz traveler symbol.

- Entertainment, nightlife and all other leisure activities are described between pages 73 and 93, while information on restaurants and cuisine is to be found on pages 94 to 101.

- Finally, there is an index at the back of the book, pp. 126–128.

Although we make every effort to ensure the accuracy of all the information in this book, changes occur incessantly. We cannot therefore take responsibility for facts, prices, addresses and circumstances in general that are constantly subject to alteration. Our guides are updated on a regular basis as we reprint, and we are always grateful to readers who let us know of any errors, changes or serious omissions they come across.

Text: Don Larrimore
Photography: Daniel Vittet
We wish to thank the Guadeloupe and Martinique Tourist Offices for their valuable assistance in the preparation of this book.
4 Cartography: 🅕🅐🅛🅚 Falk-Verlag, Hamburg.

Contents

The Islands and the People   6

A Brief History   13

Where to Go

	Guadeloupe	25
	Les Saintes	42
	Marie-Galante and Désirade	45
	Martinique	47
	Saint-Martin	63
	Saint-Barthélemy	69

What to Do

	Sports	73
	Shopping	82
	Local Culture and Events	87
	Nightlife	92

Wining and Dining   94

FWI: Facts and Figures   102

Blueprint for a Perfect Trip (Practical Information)   103

Index   126

Maps

	French West Indies	8
	Guadeloupe	24
	Martinique	46
	Saint-Martin	64
	Saint-Barthélemy	69

The Islands
and the People

They're French, indisputably—spiced with an intriguing Caribbean flavor. These perpetually sunny islands are also very beautiful in the best tropical manner: a riot of flowers, tangled green forests, mountain waterfalls, dramatic rocky headlands, beaches of white, tan or black volcanic sand. And the sunsets are breathtaking.

Each of the islands has an Atlantic and a Caribbean shore, with the water's hues spanning

a mini-spectrum from pale green to midnight blue. In the sparkling, unpolluted sea, fishing techniques haven't changed much since Columbus claimed these remote outposts for Spain almost 500 years ago.

Ashore, fields of sugarcane and banana plantations drape steep hills and rolling plains. Volcanoes, hummingbirds, mangroves, mongooses and palm trees complete the picture. The heat is year-round (average 77° F), but so are the trade winds that temper it.

On these outdoor islands, breezes are balmy, bananas are bountiful.

Anguilla (GB)

Saint-Martin (F)
Sint-Maarten (NL)

Saint-Barthélemy (F)

Sint-Eustatius (NL)

Barbuda (GB)

Saint Kitts (GB)

Nevis (GB)

Antigua (GB)

ATLANTIC

OCEAN

Montserrat (GB)

Caribbean Sea

La Désirade (F)

Guadeloupe (F)

Pointe-à-Pitre

Les Saintes (F)

Marie-Galante (F)

Dominica

N

0   50   100 km
0   50 miles

Martinique (F)
Fort-de-France

"Our little corner in the Caribbean" crows the publicity from Paris. Actually, the French West Indies (FWI)—or Antilles Françaises as they're called in France—are not at all a neat geographical cluster. The few dozen islands and rocks are widely scattered along the great curving chain of the Lesser Antilles.

Guadeloupe and Martinique, much the largest of the islands and about 100 miles apart, **8** are becoming internationally

known resorts. To the north, little Saint-Barthélemy and the French side of Saint-Martin (the other side is Dutch) have as much charm without the bustle. Though some 160 miles away, they're dependencies of Guadeloupe. So are the tiny eastern and southern satellites of Désirade, Marie-Galante and Les Saintes.

All of the islands are officially and proudly part of France, not colonies as they were for some three centuries. Martinique and Guadeloupe, formal *départements* since 1946, have recently become *régions* in an administrative reshuffle. Each has a *préfet* named in Paris, and sends three deputies and two senators more than 4,000 miles to sit in the national legislature. To New York, about 1,900 miles away, they send back streams of contented tourists.

French Antilles citizens enjoy the same state benefits as all Frenchmen, drink the same famous wines, eat the same cheeses and pâtés on *baguettes* just as crustily delicious as those turned out by every bakery in the *métropole*. And yet, despite the flocks of familiar

Sample a colorful and flavorful slice of life at outdoor markets.

French automobiles with yellow headlights, the francs and centimes, the gendarmes, cafés and Parisian-like little shops, you'll sense immediately that this isn't, nor could it ever be, metropolitan France.

The atmosphere is richer, more exotic: Africans, Asians, Indians and whites of various origins have become absorbed and transformed into the fascinating culture known as Creole. By world standards this racially varied society is a model of harmony.

What will strike you first is the marvelous range of subtly different skin tones and facial features. The famous FWI women, inevitably wearing bright earrings and flashing colors, manage to be both graceful and sensuous as they walk. This is true even when they glide along country roads with large bundles balanced on their heads. Little girls learn this sure-fire posture-improver very early in life—and there are a great many little girls.

In these already overpopulated islands, where Roman Catholicism is the predominant religion, the government provides an initial lump sum for each birth and a monthly support grant, *allocation familiale,* for each child. Because of the male exodus to France

and elsewhere in search of jobs, women continue to outnumber men; more than half of 650,000 native islanders are children and the mother is traditionally responsible for bringing them up, handling the money and making key domestic decisions.

Everyone agrees there's a special magic to the Creole soul. Smiling readily but somewhat shy about making the first approach, the islanders will often overwhelm you with kindness once contact is made. Honesty is taken for granted. You'll find a simplicity, a lack of complication, about many local people, yet something, too, of the sophistication associated with the French.

Away from tourist resorts and shopping areas, rarely will any language be spoken except French and the mystifying Creole patois, which, though based on French, is almost incomprehensible to anyone not used to it—even non-initiated Frenchmen. But people of all ages will invariably go out of their way to help a foreigner. The biggest *marque d'attention* a tourist can receive is to be invited to a Creole home.

Music goes with everything in the FWI—these are young Evangelists.

You'll soon notice how easy it is to get a cheerful early start on these islands; punch, the ubiquitous drink of local rum, sugarcane syrup and lime, is popular from dawn to dusk. And along with punch, gossiping is a favorite pastime in the FWI. The women and girls washing clothes along the river banks are probably doing that — if they're not singing. And it's a safe bet that in the open-air markets, the salesladies under the big straw hats are gossiping — between transactions involving such prized local items as guavas, tamarinds, red pimentos and green bananas.

While tropical fruits and vegetables abound, along with a satisfying variety of fresh fish, much food in the FWI is imported, primarily from France. Nowhere else in the Caribbean can you eat as imaginatively— or as well. Traditional French dishes are as highly esteemed as the spicy specialties of Creole cuisine.

As on most tropical islands, the pace of life tends to be lazy. During the hottest hours, things come to a virtual standstill, though the Caribbean siesta is an hour or two shorter than its Mediterranean counterpart. It would be folly for a visitor to expect American-style efficiency or speedy service; it would be wisest to slip into the casual drift of things West Indian. Whether eating, touring or shopping, taking your time will always be rewarding.

But when the sun goes down and the music starts up, there's nothing lazy about the dancing. This is where the *biguine* began and still belongs, along with all manner of other Caribbean rhythms just as popular and even more frenzied.

They say that if you can understand the dancing, you'll have begun to understand the Creole soul. It's certainly worth trying.

Not fully "discovered" and certainly unspoiled, the FWI are relative newcomers on the world tourist scene. Though their economic well-being is about the most precarious of any part of France, these basically agricultural islands can and do provide the scenery, the sun, the sea and the sand in sufficient quantity to attract rapidly growing numbers of vacationers looking for fun, relaxation and... something different.

Sprouting trees instead of sails,
12 *a windmill recalls sugarcane era.*

A Brief History

The appeal of the French West Indies today is that nothing much happens on them. Not so in the "bad old days." Unlikely as it seems now, at one time these sugar islands were close to center stage as the great powers of Europe warred fiercely for world commercial domination. France knew a good thing when she seized one — but then so did Britain.

It all began much more peacefully. Perhaps 2,000 years ago, Indians sometimes called Saloides from the Orinoco basin in South America began migrating up the Antilles chain, reaching Martinique and Guadeloupe before A.D. 200. A volcanic eruption on Martinique prevented these early island-hoppers from staying long; they soon vanished from history, leaving only the scantiest archaeological traces.

By A.D. 300, a new and larger wave of Amerindians from the Orinoco basin settled on islands throughout the Caribbean. These were the Arawaks, who lived from fishing and planting, and produced beautiful pottery. For centuries these people had the islands to themselves.

Then came the Caribs, and the tranquillity was shattered.

These Indians, also from South America, swept north in fast seagoing canoes, attacking and either eating or driving Arawak men off island after island and appropriating their women. A ritualistic mark of bravery for Carib warriors was cannibalism and it's for this that history most remembers the Indians who invented the hammock and gave their name to the Caribbean. In fact, their staple diet usually consisted of fish, crabs, conch and birds.

Enter Europe

On his second voyage to what he evidently thought were the islands of the Far East, Christopher Columbus in 1493 first discovered Dominica. Then he stopped at Marie-Galante, which he named after one of his vessels, before crossing over to the large neighboring island. This he called Guadeloupe, after a monastery in Spain.

The Caribs here, expert with bow and arrow, were demonstrably displeased to see the explorer. But he stayed long enough to see his first parrots and to marvel at the fact that the Indians spoke three languages — one strictly between the warriors, another for the mostly Arawak women and a third for ordinary communication between men and women.

Sailing north to find and claim islands for the Spanish crown, Columbus named one Saint-Barthélemy after his brother and another Saint-Martin, probably after the saint on whose feast day he had spotted it. Not until his fourth transatlantic journey in 1502 did Columbus reach Martinique.

Spain in the 16th century wasn't very excited about the Lesser Antilles. The big prize was gold, particularly in South America, so for a while Madrid regarded the Caribbean chain as "islands of Peru" where the galleons could stop for fresh water. Two rather half-hearted Spanish attempts to establish footholds on Guadeloupe were repulsed by the Caribs.

But as the years went by, the conquistadors rounded up even more Indians to work in gold mines elsewhere. They also introduced sugarcane, some European vegetables and the pig to the islands, but never founded any significant settlements. That situation, plus the gradual decline of Spanish naval power, proved very tempting to others.

Cardinal Richelieu, the powerful 17th-century French statesman, for one, dreamed of conquest in the New World. At his bidding, French buccaneers and adventurers, some of them noblemen, started planting the flag on Caribbean real estate in 1625. At first they shared a base with Englishmen on St. Kitts (then called Saint-Christophe). Their leader was the Norman gentleman Pierre Belain d'Esnambuc, whose statue you can see in the main square of Fort-de-France.

Some years later, French colonizers moved south to both Guadeloupe and Martinique. Liénard de l'Olive and Jean Duplessis d'Ossonville put ashore at Pointe-Allègre in northern Guadeloupe on June

Columbus plans another trip; on his second he found Guadeloupe.

28, 1635. But it took until 1640 for the French settlers to prevail against the Caribs fighting to retain the island they loved.

In September 1635, d'Esnambuc led a party to Martinique and constructed Fort Saint-Pierre where a town of that name stands today. Here too, the Caribs resisted savagely, with the result that for some 20 years they were left the eastern section of the island. It wasn't all warfare — the Indians taught the settlers fishing and weaving techniques still in use today. Finally the Caribs were expelled from the French domain, remaining for a period on Dominica and St. Vincent. In 1648, the French staked a claim to their part of Saint-Martin and to nearby Saint-Barthélemy.

Sugar and Slaves

Sugar cropping, destined to change the face and fate of the Caribbean, began booming as early as the 1640s. To work plantations on the French islands — as well as those belonging to other European nations — slaves were shipped in from Africa. The traffic soared incredibly: by 1745 Martinique had 60,000 slaves and only 16,000 whites, while Guadeloupe had even more slaves and fewer whites. Some of the slaves were able to gain freedom in return for special services rendered. The children of *colons* and slaves were free citizens.

By 1674, when Louis XIV took formal control of the islands from the debt-ridden commercial administrators, Martinique had become France's colonial capital in the Lesser

Antilles. Royal rule was to last for more than a century, with West Indian sugar helping to catapult France to economic supremacy in Europe.

Pierre Belain d'Esnambuc (left) led French colonialization. FWI guns have been silent 200 years.

Britain versus France

This was the period when nautical marauders variously called buccaneers, corsairs, privateers or pirates stalked the shipways and bays of the Caribbean. For undermanned Guadeloupe and Martinique, the French pirates were critically important: in return for a safe haven, they carried in supplies, raided enemy merchant vessels and joined battles against invading forces.

France's enemy number one in the Caribbean, as elsewhere, was the British. The first naval attacks by the redcoats were against Guadeloupe in 1691 and 1703. Half a century of fighting followed, with blockades, slave-raiding forays against the major islands and three short seizures of Saint-Martin.

During the Seven Years' War (1756–63), the British conquered Guadeloupe and held it for four years. Ironically, the **17**

British occupation gave Guadeloupe's economy a big boost: between 20,000 and 30,000 more slaves were transported in and new cane-grinding windmills built, all of which spurred the sugar trade to unprecedented prosperity. British engineers also set a port in operation at Pointe-à-Pitre, thus establishing the importance of this advantageously located town.

If there was any doubt that sugar was king in those days, the Treaty of Paris (1763) dispelled it: France elected to take back her little West Indian islands and leave the "few snowy acres" of Canada to the British!

During the American War of Independence, France's sympathies were undisguised: American ships were granted safe anchorage in the FWI, privateers raiding from Saint-Barthélemy's coves sank many a British merchantman, and a Martinique regiment fought the British at Savannah, Georgia. On April 12, 1782, in the sea channel near Guadeloupe's little off-shore islands of Les Saintes, a British fleet gained historic revenge against French

Epic naval battle was named for
18 *beautiful, tranquil Les Saintes.*

Père Labat

Dominican priest, explorer, chronicler, botanist, architect, engineer and even warrior, Père Labat, known to every French West Indian, rallied the bitter defense against Britain's assault on Guadeloupe in 1703. (His tower, which you can see at Baillif near Basse-Terre, was the key bastion.) Interrupting his research on the pre-Columbian Indians, he fought in various other battles during his 11 years in the islands. On his return to France he wrote an enormously popular book (*Nouveau Voyage aux Isles de l'Amérique*) in 1722, which remains the most detailed — if at times fanciful — account of French colonial life in the sugar era.

Admiral de Grasse, of Yorktown fame, in a battle you'll still hear about today.

De Grasse's fleet of 34 warships was escorting a convoy of 150 cargo vessels to Santo Domingo* planning to join a Spanish naval venture against Britain's base on Jamaica. British Admiral Rodney, with 37 ships and a crucial superiority in cannon (3,012 to 2,246 French), struck off Les Saintes. As the islanders watched from their hills, the more mobile British mercilessly chopped up the French convoy until finally de Grasse surrendered. This disastrous French naval defeat is known as the Battle of Les Saintes.

Slavery Declines

When, during the French Revolution, the Convention ambitiously declared slavery abolished, Martinique's wealthy plantation owners frantically objected. Opting, as a dubious second best, for eight years of British occupation in 1794, the island managed to retain slavery — and avoid the revolutionary terror which Guadeloupe underwent.

After Britain seized Guadeloupe, Victor Hugues, *commissaire* of the Convention, wrenched the island back, proclaimed slavery abolished and set about guillotining the old-guard *colons*. His corsairs became the scourge of the sea, the indiscriminate attacks leading to a diplomatic blow-up with the new American government. Hugues' reign on Guadeloupe didn't last long, but it was bloodthirsty enough to be recalled vividly even today.

In 1802 France reclaimed Martinique from Britain through the Treaty of Amiens. Bonaparte, as First Consul of

*today's Dominican Republic and Haiti.

20

France, reinstated slavery in the FWI, and historians still argue over the role played in that decision by his Creole wife Josephine, a native of Martinique (see p. 57).

Sugarcane was revered by the planters and government conservatives as "white gold" *(l'or blanc)* for the immense wealth it brought. But in 1799 doom was signaled for the cane monopoly with the appearance of the cheaper sugar beet. The end also became inevitable for the slave system upon which the sugar industry was based: the example of Santo Domingo's slave revolt, which led to the independence of a new republic named Haiti, was electrifying, causing an entirely new attitude to the whole problem of the slave trade. Liberal ideas began mushrooming in France itself and after Nelson destroyed Napoleon's fleet at the Battle of Trafalgar, the French West Indian planters' lifeline with France was all but destroyed. In addition, the Congress of Vienna formally banned the trade in slaves.

Abolition and Beyond
The stage was now set for the French West Indies' greatest hero, Victor Schoelcher. The son of a Parisian porcelain merchant, Schoelcher was inspired to wage a 15-year struggle to free the slaves by what he saw on three trips to the Caribbean.

When the Republic was proclaimed in Paris in 1848, Schoelcher drafted the emancipation decree that freed 87,500 slaves in Guadeloupe, 72,000 in Martinique. Today the smallest hamlets on both islands honor Schoelcher with busts, full statues and street names. Martinique has a town named after him.

No slaves meant almost no sugar production, until the first of some 80,000 Hindus from India and 16,000 free Africans began arriving as contract workers for Guadeloupe and Martinique plantations. Many Indians remained and established small farms in the FWI, their descendants becoming an important and colorful segment of the population (see box p. 45).

To help stimulate the economy, the islands were finally relieved of the long-standing and controversial requirement that, as colonial appendages of France, they could trade only with the French and usually only in French ships. Rum now began bringing in considerable legal (as opposed to contraband) revenue.

In 1871 under the Third Republic, Martinique and Guade- **21** loupe were granted representation in the National Assembly in Paris, which they have retained ever since. Gradually metropolitan institutions and the benefits of French citizenship were extended to the FWI.

In 1877, France bought back Saint-Barthélemy from Sweden for 320,000 gold francs (Louis XVI having ceded the little island 93 years earlier to his friend King Gustav III in return for duty-free trading rights in Gothenburg).

The 20th Century

The FWI's worst modern tragedy came in 1902 when the sophisticated city of Saint-Pierre was totally destroyed by the eruption of Mount Pelée. The victims—over 30,000—included most of Martinique's social and managerial élite. Henceforth Fort-de-France would be the island's only significant center and the largest city in the French Antilles.

When France fell in World War II, the FWI's administrator, Admiral Georges Robert, decreed allegiance to the Vichy régime, although most of the islanders were against the move. Fearing German occupation and submarine use of the islands, the Allies imposed a painful blockade and threat-

ened to use military force. In 1943 Robert resigned and the islands swung immediately to de Gaulle's Free French. With the war monopolizing shipping, the FWI suffered great economic privation.

Guadeloupe and Martinique became full *départements* of France in 1946—a source of great pride to many. More importantly, it meant much-needed, larger financial contributions from Paris. The smaller islands, French Saint-Martin and Saint-Barthélemy, are administrative sub-prefectures *(sous-préfectures)* of Guadeloupe.

While sugar, rum and banana exports resumed to a degree after the war, the islands' economies have not kept satisfactory pace with their burgeoning populations. The recent surge of tourism has helped, but not enough. Unrest and some political extremism have surfaced from time to time, but since aid from France is so vital, and French customs so ingrained, it seems almost inconceivable that the FWI will seek total independence as other Caribbean islands have done.

Loading sugarcane—the "white gold" of the French West Indies.

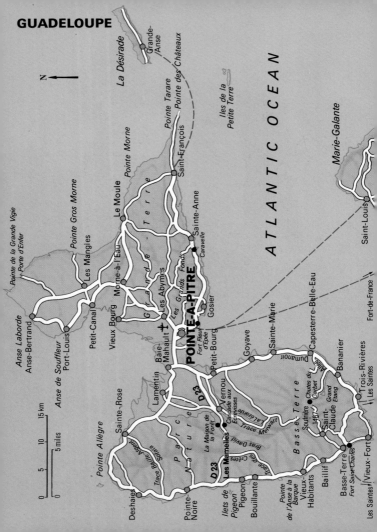

Where to Go

Guadeloupe

Proudly styling itself the Caribbean's "emerald isle," Guadeloupe is actually two islands linked by a drawbridge across the narrow, salt-water Salée River. Guadeloupe, from the air or on a map, resembles a butterfly.

This largest of the FWI spreads its wings midway along the Lesser Antilles chain. Its major neighbors are English-speaking Montserrat and Antigua to the north and Dominica to the south, the latter separating it from Martinique.

Columbus named it after his favorite Spanish monastery, Our Lady of Guadeloupe in Estremadura. To the Carib Indians then living here, it was Karukera — island of beautiful waters. You'll see why.

Between the two world wars, President Theodore Roosevelt stopped by, was entranced by "the beautiful countryside and friendly people of Guadeloupe" and predicted that thousands of American tourists would soon be visiting each winter. It took the advent of jetliners and cruise ships for that to happen.

Less conservative than Martinique, Guadeloupe of late seems to be bidding to become the nudist playground of the Caribbean. Several of its beaches are officially designated for nudism (known locally as *naturisme*), and a functionary who is a Chevalier de la Légion d'Honneur has been appointed to supervise all aspects of sunning in the buff.

Guadeloupe's two component islands are notably dissimilar and confusingly named. Grande-Terre (Great Land) is smaller (218 square miles), drier, flatter and more important because it has Pointe-à-Pitre, Guadeloupe's commercial center and largest city. Basse-Terre (Low Land), is higher, bigger (312 square miles), greener and has the political capital, also called Basse-Terre, which is near the famous will-it-or-won't-it Soufrière volcano. The islands' names refer to the different force winds hitting them, not their topography.

About 350,000 people live on Guadeloupe with some 30,000 on its administrative dependencies (Saint-Martin, Saint-Barthélemy, Marie-Galante, Les Saintes and Désirade). Two-thirds are classified as mulattoes, including some 16,000 Asian Indians. Blacks form 27 per cent of the population, and **25**

Creole whites born here, 8 per cent. The high population density constitutes a real problem.

Scattered around Guadeloupe are some 50 stately Creole-style plantation homes of wood and stone, recalling the distant days of sugar prosperity. You're also likely to see modest modern houses being transported from place to place on flat trucks—Guadeloupeans, who don't always own land, like to move around.

Sight-seeing for tourists is most rewarding by rental car, boat or both. Otherwise, hotels offer guided tours to scenic points. Small local buses or collective taxis are inexpensive and useful for point-to-point travel (complete with transistor music and happy humanity), but not for general touring. Guadeloupe's ordinary taxis may also be hired, but are extremely expensive.

Pointe-à-Pitre

When this city was only a tiny fishing village three centuries ago, a Dutchman named Pieter is said to have been the most popular fish peddler at a jetty on the waterfront. Even though he wasn't French, from Pieter the name Pointe-à-Pitre was eventually derived.

Today weathered banana schooners chug past yachts and gargantuan passenger liners to dock in this curious tropical port which is Guadeloupe's principal city and gateway to the world. A formless amalgam of wooden shacks and modern apartment buildings, Oriental-style bazaars and shopping-center supermarkets, Pointe-à-Pitre betrays little of its turbulent past. The traffic jams seem incongruous, but they're authentic. Half a day should allow the tourist ample time for city sight-seeing and shopping.

Don't miss the **open-air market** close by the wharves. This is the West Indies at their most colorful. Aside from exotic fruits, strange roots, land crabs, dried fish, spices and nuts, you can pick up "spiritual spray" for your house, ointments designed to bring you money, lotions and powders for your ailments or a baby pig. Some of the stands under the gay umbrellas are real herbalists' heavens; but even if you can understand the patois, it's difficult to learn the precise uses for certain mysterious-looking items.

Close by (nothing that matters in Pointe-à-Pitre is far away) is the center of youthful social "action"—the Place de

la Victoire sprawling in the shade of sandbox trees. During one phase of the French Revolution, a guillotine shortened many lives here, though the fact is deliberately forgotten by the boys eyeing the girls pretending to ignore the boys. Just off this pleasant main square of the city, you'll find the useful state tourist office (Office du Tourisme).

Pointe-à-Pitre's cathedral, the **Basilique Saint-Pierre et Saint-Paul** features unusual metal columns and balconies. It was the creation, in 1873, of a certain Monsieur Trouille (Mr. "Jitters"). Destroyed by three hurricanes in this century

Using their heads, Guadeloupe ladies solve transport problems.

and rebuilt each time, the church is now said to be almost entirely constructed of pieces of iron. Its simple beauty is enhanced by locally designed stained-glass windows in red, blue, orange and yellow. The church is on Place Gourbeyre, opposite the modest Palais de Justice and just a few steps from the city's main shopping district which embraces rues Nozières, Frébault and Schoelcher.

Wandering in these fascinating little streets is best in the **27** early morning or late afternoon when the crowds and heat are reduced. You'll see dozens of iron-grilled buildings reminiscent of that other former French colonial port, New Orleans, Louisiana.

The almost midtown Massabielle quarter *(faubourg de Massabielle)*, is sometimes described as the most "picturesque" in the city. It's a warren of wooden and corrugated-iron cabins, housing a remarkable number of people. Discretion when using your camera is advisable here.

Around Grande-Terre

Three formidable cannons greet you at the wooden drawbridge entrance to **Fort Fleur d'Epée** which commands access to Pointe-à-Pitre's harbor. It's a 10-minute drive from the city.

Late in the 18th century, British and French forces fought bloody hand-to-hand battles for this strategic hill considered the key to the defense of all Guadeloupe. Today birds chirp in the flamboyant trees at this totally tranquil spot. In the dungeon-like chambers of the fort's lower reaches, relics and documents relating to the war were kept in a decorated room until the prevailing humidity destroyed them and it was closed to the public.

A little past the small theater built for local dramatic performances, there's a fine view across the bay to Basse-Terre.

A few miles down the coast at **Gosier,** although it's difficult to imagine, contingents of fierce invaders used to put ashore. Today this is Guadeloupe's "riviera," with resort hotels strung along the beaches and tennis courts laid out among the coconut trees.

To reach Gosier's attractive offshore islet, it's a challenging swim or an easy boat ride. Beneath the small lighthouse on this uninhabited speck of sand and trees, picnicking and nude bathing are popular pastimes. Windsurfers and sailboats on the aquamarine waters make a memorable Caribbean snapshot (best from the hillside village of Gosier itself). Here, in the heart of the island's tourist area, you'll find a number of small Creole, French and Oriental restaurants and a few discotheques.

Near the pleasant seaside village of **Sainte-Anne** further east is what is generally considered to be Guadeloupe's best beach. If you land by boat,

Music is certainly the food of friendship on a Caribbean beach.

Cleaning and mending fishing nets involves an exercise in patience.

Caravelle beach is yours for the using; otherwise you'll have to pay a nominal charge to the vacation club that owns the acreage. A sizable segment of this long curving beach of white sand is devoted to *naturisme*; almost everywhere else on the entire strand, toplessness holds sway in the current French fashion, but nobody insists on it.

Sainte-Anne itself has a long, broad beach used not only by fishermen in vividly painted boats, but also by families with small children. The village was named after the wife of King Louis XIII, Queen Anne of Austria.

Inland from both Gosier and Sainte-Anne is a peaceful region of green hills, or *mornes* as they're known in the West Indies. Few of the tiny settlements identify themselves with signs; roads are generally unmarked, and it can therefore be somewhat bewildering. But you can't get lost for long, and in perhaps half an hour of driving around this area of **Grands Fonds** you'll get a real feeling for the pastoral simplicity that's typical of Guadeloupe. On the narrow roads that tend to twist without warning, you'll encounter cows, sheep, sugarcane wagons and little children.

Back on the coast, **Saint-François** is a delightful fishing village. At any hour of the day you'll see lobster traps being put together and nets being mended along the shore. An even more picturesque scene is when the boats come in and jostling housewives buy the day's catch direct from the fishermen.

From Saint-François an excessively narrow road heads straight to the easternmost point of Guadeloupe (30 miles from Pointe-à-Pitre)—and one of the scenic highlights of the entire Caribbean. This is the **Pointe des Châteaux,** a wildly beautiful cliff formation with rocks shaped like castles lashed and eroded by the Atlantic's waves. You may well get sprinkled by sea spray as you walk along the rocky bluff to the large cement cross erected (between 1947 and 1951) at the summit. Don't fail to go all the way. From this spectacular point, the view is outstanding. The large island in the distance is Désirade, the small Petite-Terre islets are much closer.

A short distance off the road on the way to Pointe des Châteaux, the long TARARE BEACH is another favorite with nudists.

A pre-columbian Arawak Indian village has been unearthed near the once-flourishing sugar town of LE MOULE. Resort hotels in the area take advantage of several sandy beaches protected by breakwaters from the heavy Atlantic surf that pounds most of Grande-Terre's east coast. Most dramatic is the northern **Porte d'Enfer** (Gate of Hell), where the waves have sliced a huge chasm into the limestone shoreline. At the innermost point where the ocean's force is completely spent but the booming waves can still be heard is a small beach with shaded picnic area adjoining it.

The sparsely inhabited northern part of Grande-Terre is sugarcane and cattle country. Notice the windmills, mostly in ruins, that once ground cane.

At the end of a bumpy dirt road as far north as you can go in Guadeloupe is the magnificent **Pointe de la Grande Vigie.** For a picnic or simply to contemplate nature's wonders, this spot is unbeatable. Follow the signs to the sightseeing point where, on the predictably clear day, you can see across 30 miles of blue ocean to Désirade, 42 miles to Antigua and even 48 miles to the green peaks of Montserrat. Below, you'll hear the waves crashing into caves worn into the cliffsides. This is a place where you'll exult in being alive.

On a spur-road just a little north of the sleepy village of ANSE BERTRAND is the ANSE LABORDE, a public beach of tan sand with gorgeous turquoise waters and good snorkeling off rocky promontories. Further south at the fishing village of PORT-LOUIS, you can drive right to one of the island's best beaches, **Anse de Souffleur.**

From Port-Louis all the way down Grande Terre's west coast to Pointe-à-Pitre there extend vast mangrove swamps. They're almost unreachable except by boat, but rewarding for fishermen and birdwatchers. The main highway south passes through the towns of PETIT CANAL and MORNE-À-L'EAU, both characteristic of rural, agricultural Guadeloupe, and through Pointe-à-Pitre's heavily populated satellite district of LES ABYMES.

Around Basse-Terre

An undulating coastal highway completely encircles this mountainous and densely forested island, but it's much too long a trip to make comfortably in one day. Among the best excursions is one over another good road, D 23, directly through the Natural Park which covers more than 74,000 acres of Basse-Terre's interior. This **"cross-country highway"** *(La Traversée)* continues west just beyond the breezy hilltop

Pointe de la Grande Vigie offers outstanding Guadeloupe seascapes.

village of VERNOU. Here, overlooking the Lézarde river valley with its swaying sugarcane, are elaborate secluded villas which seem a universe apart from the small sheds in which most Guadeloupeans live. As you drive along the winding road up to Vernou, notice the trees with huge, weird roots.

In Guadeloupe's tropical rain forest, it's worth stopping each time a wooden sign announces a particular attraction. The rustic **Bras-David picnic area,** for example, is set alongside a burbling stream. At the **House of the Forest** (*La Maison de la Forêt*), there's an audio-visual exhibit (in French only), and you can take any of three guided walks along "discovery trails" (*sentiers de découverte*) lasting 10, 20 or 60 minutes. For serious hikers, there are other major trails in the park.

It's only a few hundred yards from the highway along a fern-lined path to the **Crayfish Falls** (*Cascade aux Ecrevisses*), a paradisiacal "swimming hole" to splash around in. If you're lucky, nobody else will be there to enjoy the waterfall, the rocks and ferns and the picnic site. You'll see a sign announcing that there are 1,500 types of flora in Guadeloupe and just off the road you'll find a nursery that sells specimens.

Reassuring note: Unlike Martinique, Guadeloupe has no poisonous snakes or other harmful animals.

On this road, the highest point comes at the PASS OF THE TWO BREASTS (*Les Deux Mamelles*), altitude 1,969 feet, where it's worth stopping for the view. For more sweeping panoramas, you can hike for less than an hour to either summit—Petit-Bourg (2,349 ft.) or Pigeon (2,526 ft.).

For those not spending the

entire day in the park, it's possible to return to Pointe-à-Pitre by circling the northern section of Basse-Terre along the coast road. On the leeward coast, underwater sportsmen can head for the simple fishing village of PIGEON to pick up a boat to the tiny Ilet de Pigeon. Otherwise, you drive north through POINTE-NOIRE (named for its black volcanic hillsides) and DESHAIES, an unexceptional town on a very beautiful bay. Continuing on, you'll reach the much-admired surfing beach at **Grande Anse,** where fine brown sand slopes away from palm trees to green-blue water. If you've brought lunch, Grande Anse has pleasant shoreside picnic spots.

Further on you come to SAINTE-ROSE. Here in the 17th century the first French landing party under Duplessis ran into

Socializing goes with the soaping at the scenic natural laundromats.

violent and unfriendly Caribs. Today it's a drowsily peaceful fishing village. On its outskirts the road crosses a river where you may see children fishing or swimming off flat rocks, and women and girls washing clothes—as they do in all 14 of Basse-Terre's major rivers.

Along the way back through LAMENTIN to the Pointe-à-Pitre expressway you'll pass seemingly endless fields of unusually tall sugarcane.

South to Soufrière

From Pointe-à-Pitre, thick groves of banana trees with the fruit protected from insects by transparent bags and fields of sugarcane stretch away from the southbound coastal highway through PETIT-BOURG and GOYAVE. You're now approaching the spot where Europeans first encountered Guadeloupe late in the 15th century. But if you're not watching closely, you may miss the unprepossessing bust of Christopher Columbus perched atop a column in a little roadside square. The village is SAINTE-MARIE, named by the

The exhilarating Carbet falls are a little-known Caribbean delight— the children, a well-known one.

explorer when he landed on November 4, 1493, attracted by the waterfalls and river he could see flowing down the green inland mountains. On the base of the white bust, erected in 1916, there's a declaration in French that it was here that Karukera became Guadeloupe.

Just past the attractive farming town of CAPESTERRE, the highway becomes, for about 1½ miles, the so-called **Allée Dumanoir.** Twin rows of majestic royal palm trees line the road. Behind them are vast groves of banana trees.

A bit further along you'll certainly want to turn off the

Those curious enough to walk down the rural road to the seacoast will find pigs, goats, chickens and children but no likely looking landing place for a boat. Locals shrug and suggest that the shoreline's topography must have changed in the 500 years since Columbus.

coast road and head up to the **Carbet falls.** First you wind through dense banana plantations, then ferns and tree vines, and then as the road narrows to a cement track, the tropical foliage closes in. Civilization here seems very distant. To reach any of the three Carbet falls, you must continue walk-

ing after the roads come to an end—for 20 minutes, 30 minutes or two hours respectively. Signs direct you to these great waterfalls which are among Guadeloupe's finest, if least-visited, scenic attractions.

Just off the road (D4) to the falls is the **Grand Etang,** a placid lake surrounded by forest with silence broken only by birds, insects and fish that occasionally flip out of the water. It takes less than an hour to stroll all the way round the pleasant path surrounding the water.

Back on the coastal highway, you won't wonder why the village of BANANIER has its name. From here to Trois-Rivières is one of the loveliest drives in the FWI. At the lookout point, pull over for an inviting panorama of the offshore islands of Les Saintes.

At **Trois-Rivières,** stop to see fascinating rock engravings believed carved about 1,600 years ago by the Arawak Indians. A delightful **archaeological park** has been created on the hillside around these huge, mysterious rocks. The inscriptions seem to be more than casual etchings,

but their significance isn't known. Three rocks have been removed to museums in Berlin, New York and Paris; others in the Trois-Rivières area outside the park have not yet been classified as historical monuments by the French government. Local residents will tell you where to find them. Brochures in English, available without charge, describe the rocks and vegetation.

Down the road from the archaeological park is a lively covered fish and vegetable market. From the cement jetty here, boats leave early every morning for Les Saintes.

Guadeloupe's political capital, **Basse-Terre,** is much smaller and sleepier than Pointe-à-Pitre. Just passing through, you may be reminded of a minor town in the French provinces—except for its magnificent seaside setting at the foot of **Mount Soufrière's** green slopes. The mighty Fort Saint-Charles dates back to 1645. If you do stop in Basse-Terre, you might like to spend some time at the large market just off the capital's broad shoreline drive.

From here it's all up: through the charming hillside village of **Saint-Claude,** with its upper-income residences and clinics, and on toward the summit—or

Trois-Rivières petroglyphs may be perplexing, but foliage is labeled.

39

It huffs, puffs and occasionally even blows a bit. No one gets hurt. Practically all of Guadeloupe's tourist hotels are far out of range. La Soufrière, temperamental and magnificent even if its peak is almost always shrouded in clouds, is a "semi-active" volcano. At 4,813 feet, it dominates the lush and rugged south of Basse Terre. When it began acting up with low-grade "vapor explosions" in the summer of 1976, alarming headlines appeared in papers worldwide. 72,000 volcano-zone residents were evacuated at great cost to the French government. But nothing more happened, and people gradually returned home. Soufrière is a splendid and perfectly safe place to visit—otherwise the monitoring experts wouldn't let you go.

as far as the gendarmes are allowing traffic to proceed that day. The higher you go, the more sulphur you'll smell, from bubbling fissures in an eerily beautiful landscape. A scenic but rather narrow road skirts Soufrière's cone and the Carbet falls on the other side of the volcano. You can drive almost to the crater, but you have to climb the final 1,000 feet to the top (don't forget to bring along a sweater). On cloudless days, a spectacular panorama awaits you. But wherever you are on the mountain's upper reaches, the views are glorious. To appreciate the hiking trails here, an excellent Natural Park booklet available in English can be obtained from the Tourist Office in Pointe-à-Pitre.

From Basse-Terre north, the leeward coast *(côte sous le vent)* has a few small beaches of black volcanic sand and some picturesque paraphernalia of the fishermen who favor these waters. Outside BAILLIF is the best preserved of the sugar-mill watchtowers erected by the famous militant priest, Père Labat (see p. 20). It saw bloody fighting between the French and English at the beginning of the 18th century. One of Guadeloupe's prettiest bays is **Anse à la Barque** (Boat Cove), so-named because fishing boats have long ridden out storms in its protected anchorage.

The earth lets off steam on semi-active La Soufrière's wild slopes.

Les Saintes

You might pack a toothbrush as well as your bathing suit if you decide on a one-day excursion to this cluster of little islands—they're hard to leave. Only two of the eight islands are inhabited, and one, TERRE DE BAS, just barely. You'll land at the main island, **Terre de Haut,** after either a 15-minute small-plane flight from Pointe-à-Pitre or a 40-minute splashy motor launch trip from Trois-Rivières.

The harbor here, dotted with yachts and fishing boats, is reminiscent of a mini-Rio de Janeiro or various Aegean and Mediterranean ports. Red-roofed houses nestle on the surrounding hills. Under a trim white beacon, a sign says: *"Terre de Haut est heureuse de vous accueillir et vous souhaite un agréable séjour"* (Terre de Haut is happy to welcome you and wishes you a pleasant stay). They mean it. Little children carrying trays offer you coconut tarts—a filling treat for a franc or two. And everybody seems to be similing.

You'll soon notice that this is first and foremost a fishing island—nets, lobster traps, gutting knives, rods and lines are everywhere; it's no surprise to learn that the inhabitants, mostly descendants of Bretons who settled here 300 years ago, are considered the best fishermen in the Antilles. Both they and their long bright boats are called Saintois. The islanders often wear a distinctively flat hat known as a *salako* and don't mind being photographed by polite visitors.

To begin with, you can take a guided minibus tour (local drivers generally speak French only), that covers all three miles of road on the island. It includes hilltop Fort Napoléon, unscathed since it was built after the days of Anglo-French warfare in the region. (Some modern art work is displayed inside.) On the Cabrit islet across the way you'll see a 19th-century fort named, inevitably, after the Empress Josephine.

After strolling for the five minutes it takes to examine the little village, wise tourists head directly for **Pont-Pierre beach** (there's a nominal admission charge). This might be your idea of paradise: a semicircular sandy strip backed by sea grapes and tropical shrubs, gentle aquamarine surf, a coral reef close

A cluttered beach by Les Saintes standards—bathers go elsewhere.

to shore plus some rocks and seaweed for rewarding snorkeling and a view out to some huge "pierced rocks" *(roches percées)* that partly shelter the entrance to the cove.

There's more shade, from coconut trees, at the delightful unnamed beach on the little **Pain de Sucre peninsula** across the island. Among other beach possibilities is ANSE CRAWEN which is a *naturisme* haunt and said to offer the best off-the-beach snorkeling and skin diving. Underwater exploring in the transparent depths of the Les Saintes archipelago ranges from good to outstanding. For a negotiable sum, boatmen will take you around the isles, pointing out where the great 1782 naval encounter occurred between French and British fleets, known as the Battle of Les Saintes (see pp. 18–20).

Terre de Haut has several places to stay, but book ahead, particularly on weekends. At the handful of restaurants, the fare unfailingly features the freshest possible fish.

Note: It costs about four times as much to fly to and from Les Saintes as to make the round-trip sea journey. Boats set sail from Trois-Rivières (30 miles from Pointe-à-Pitre), Basse-Terre and Pointe-à-Pitre.

Marie-Galante and Désirade

Most tourists won't want to take time on a limited vacation to visit these island dependencies of Guadeloupe. There are, however, regular small-plane flights to both islands and less recommended runs by boat.

MARIE-GALANTE, large and round and noted for the rum from its extensive sugarcane fields, was named by Columbus after the ship that brought him across the Atlantic on his second voyage. The island has a number of fine white-sand beaches, notably La Feuillère near Capesterre, Vieux Fort and Folle Anse. There is also an attractive 18th-century residence called Château Murat.

The atmosphere is simple and relaxed, the people very kind, the Creole food good (try *bébélé*, an African-style soup of many ingredients including breadfruit, crabs, bananas and peas).

Beautiful beaches lure the determined few off the beaten path to DÉSIRADE—its name

A Touch of India

Not the least of the many surprises in the FWI is the number of Asian Indians you'll notice. Guadeloupe has about 16,000 of these handsome people, Martinique fewer. They're immediately recognizable though saris and turbans are rarely seen nowadays. These are descendants of the contract workers recruited from the Asian subcontinent last century to replace the liberated slaves on sugar plantations. A few have married outside their race—the blend of Indian and African is strikingly attractive. Though most now are Roman Catholic, the Indians still sacrifice goats or sheep at the culmination of traditional rituals you're welcome to watch. These take place at small temples. One major Indian center is Matouba high on La Soufrière; others are at Fond-Saint-Denis, Basse-Pointe and on the road to Saint-Pierre on Martinique. Skilled in working the soil, the Indians are Guadeloupe's most important vegetable gardeners.

signifying yearned-for land. This was the first of the Antilles spotted by Columbus in 1493.

If you like early nights and lazy days, you'll enjoy Désirade, home to 1,600 farmers and fishermen.

45

Pointe-à-Pitre

ATLANTIC

N

Grande-Rivière   Macouba
              Basse-Pointe

Le Lorrain

Anse Céron
Anse Belleville
Montagne Pelée
1397
Le Prêcheur

Ajoupa
Bouillon

Le Morne Rouge

Sainte-Marie

Pointe Caracoli

ROUTE DE LA TRACE

Saint-Pierre
Anse Turin

Fond-
Saint-Denis

Pitons
du Carbet -1120

La Trinité

presqu'île la Caravelle

OCEAN

La Carbet

Gros Morne

Bellefontaine

La Donis

Le Robert

Case-Pilote

Saint-Joseph

Caribbean

Schoelcher

Le Lamentin

Le François

FORT-DE-FRANCE

Le Saint-
Esprit   504 Mont
                Vauclin

Pointe du Bout
Anse à l'Ane
La Pagerie
*Musée
de la Pagerie*

Les
Trois Ilets

Rivière-
Salée

Le Vauclin

Sea

Rivière-
Pilote

Les Anses-d'Arlets

Le Marin

Cap Macré

Cap Ferré

Le Diamant

Sainte-Luce

Cap Cabaret

Cap Chevalier
Ilet
Hardy

Rocher du Diamant

Sainte-
Anne

Pointe Baham

*Grande Anse
des Salines*

MARTINIQUE

0   5   10   15 km

0   5   10 miles

St. Lucia

Martinique

The Indians called it *Madinina* —island of flowers, and they were right: hibiscus and bougainvillea, magnolia and oleander, anthurium, poinsettia and more, all compete to make Martinique one of the most colorful tropical gardens on earth. When Columbus discovered the island late in his career, he called it "the best, the most fertile, the sweetest, the most charming country in the world" and named it Matinino, probably after Saint Martin (or, some say, as an approximation of Madinina), a name which the French later adapted to Martinique.

This southernmost of the French West Indies lies between English-speaking Dominica and Saint Lucia. Its 425 square miles are crowded with 400,000 inhabitants. The islanders are vibrant, generous and passionate: the loveliness of Martinique's women is legendary, the number of children... astounding. Josephine, Empress of France and wife of Napoleon was born here.

Today, as always, the time-honored occupations of fishing and farming support Martinique's fragile existence—the delicious rum also helps. But, as in Guadeloupe, the economic future seems somewhat uncertain even with increasing tourism.

The visitor will most appreciate Martinique by exploring in a rented car, or if three or four people share the cost, a tour by regular taxi becomes a reasonable proposition. For tourists at hotels and for cruise ship passengers, there are also guided group excursions to major attractions by minibus or boat.

Fort-de-France

Clinging to its superb **harbor,** Martinique's capital is sometimes bustling, sometimes drowsy—but always captivating. Awesome green mountains form the backdrop while strikingly tall palm trees dwarf all but a very few buildings.

In the great bay where flying fish rise at dusk, sloops and ketches, ferry boats and freighters, cruise ships and fishing boats never have a parking problem. Ashore it's another matter, with peak-hour traffic jams and midtown parking woes.

This is a city to savor on foot. Best is the teeming shopping area centered on the **rue Isambert market.** In this cavernous emporium you'll have your pick of fresh Martinique pineapples, coconut slices or the pungent baby limes so loved in the West Indies. Among the bananas and Caribbean sweet potatoes, you'll find bottles of old-time patent medicines for sale. This delightful marketplace has its own snack bar featuring a fresh vegetable *repas* (meal) for a relatively modest amount by French West Indies standards.

The streets nearby are filled with shops selling bright material, including the madras prints so typical of the FWI, ready-made clothing, shoes and jewelry. Bargaining here could well be worthwhile.

When you reach the "canal," technically the Levassor River*, you'll want to cross over the stone footbridge. Small boats tie up here with batches of crayfish, fresh fish and eel, and housewives clamor for the fishermen to weigh their choices

* The propeller *(l'hélice)* was invented by a Martiniquais, Gilbert Canque, and tested for the first time in this rather murky stream.

on rudimentary scales. The formal **fish market** is further along the fascinating canalside Boulevard Allègre. In this enclosed but airy building, you'll find ladies with large machetes expertly chopping off hunks of kingfish, tuna or shark for eager buyers.

Tourists and Martiniquais alike tend to gravitate toward the landscaped park called **La Savane** near the water's edge in the heart of the city. Beyond the outdoor shopping pavilions

here, you'll come across a white marble statue of Napoleon's Josephine, holding a rose and facing the direction of her birthplace across the bay.

Pierre Belain d'Esnambuc, the Norman adventurer who first claimed Martinique for France, also has a statue here, but cast in less regal bronze. Though you'd never guess it, the French fought bloody battles on La Savane against the English and Dutch. Near the park, notice the New Orleans-style iron grillwork on the buildings.

Alongside La Savane runs rue de la Liberté, and at No. 9 is Martinique's excellent **Musée Départemental.** In the three stories of this little air-conditioned museum you can see displays of prehistoric Indian artifacts, skeletal bones found locally and a wealth of items chosen to evoke a feeling for the island's history over the past three centuries. Napoleon and Josephine get top billing, of course, as does the eruption of Mount Pelée (see p. 52). There are slave irons, traditional island costumes and an interesting French map of 1778

Watchful eyes and ready cash for the big one that didn't get away. **49**

showing the *théâtre de la guerre* (theater of war) between the Americans and the British. The museum is open from 9 a.m. to noon and 3 to 6 p.m. Monday to Friday (with audio-visual shows in the afternoon) and on Saturday mornings.

Further along rue de la Liberté is the startling **Schoelcher Library** *(Bibliothèque)*. This odd but attractive town house, with its collection of Arawak and Carib relics, was on display at the 1889 Paris Exposition, then dismantled, brought to Martinique and reconstructed. Recently quite some restoration has been done to the Library, as it has to another midtown Fort-de-France landmark, the **Saint-Louis Cathedral** of 1895, which has undergone total reconstruction.

You'll have to confine your viewing to the outside of that old citadel in the harbor, **Fort Saint-Louis,** unless you're able to obtain special visitor's permission from the French military (true of all Martinique's forts). In the 17th century this fort was all there was to the town, but dwellings were gradually built up around it on reclaimed marshland. The fort, which held off a savage Dutch attack in 1674, was known as Fort-Royal, later corrupted in Creole to *Foyal*. Napoleon named it Fort-de-France and that name was taken over for the town. Fires and hurricanes during the last century subsequently reduced its importance. Had it not been for the volcanic disaster that all but wiped Saint-Pierre off the map in 1902, Fort-de-France would never have become Martinique's leading city.

Fabulous Ferry
Frequent, comfortable ferries link the capital with the Pointe du Bout hotel area across the bay, a 20-minute ride of pure pleasure. Smaller launches run regular services to slightly more distant beach areas. Local commuters seem oblivious to the view. But unless you have your own sailboat, the deck of a ferry is the best place to appreciate this marvelous Caribbean harbor. The most satisfying time is late any breezy afternoon toward sunset (which comes with surprising swiftness in the West Indies at about 6 p.m.). Standing on the deck here and watching the sun go down may well make you feel that life's really wonderful—after all!

Sundown heralds funtime in Fort-de-France, Martinique's capital.

51

Venture Into the Interior

If you have time for only one road trip on the island, be sure it includes the **Route de la Trace**, more prosaically known as Route Nationale 3. La Trace is one of the Caribbean's great roads, with gorgeous views down into ravines and up at the deep green Carbet peaks that dominate north-central Martinique. Along the way, near the hamlet of LA DONIS, there are two thriving nurseries which sell local foliage species but note that these are closed on Sundays.

Caution: Unlike other FWI islands, Martinique has poisonous snakes, and walking off a marked forest trail is not recommended.

For that out-of-this-world feeling and superior tropical mountain scenery, try first gear on the road to **Fond-Saint-Denis.** Precipitous turns lead to the observatory of the University of Paris, strategically perched to monitor the Pelée volcano. To visit this establishment, which resembles a private residence, you must make arrangements three days in advance. Up here, gazing out at strikingly lush mountains, you may find yourself higher than the clouds, which adds to the extraordinary eerie atmosphere of the place.

Saint-Pierre and the Volcano

It was a lovely seaside town, the first French settlement on Martinique and, by early 1902, so culturally and economically thriving that it was nicknamed the "Paris of the West Indies." When 4,700-foot Mount Pelée began belching smoke and cinders far above Saint-Pierre in late April, which it had done harmlessly before, authorities professed no concern. Evacuation was unthinkable—an election was coming up.

On May 4–5 a mass of mud and rocks was swept down by Pelée's White River *(Rivière Blanche)* over a factory, killing 25 people. At the same time a tidal wave lashed the shores near Saint-Pierre. Flames began spouting from the mountain's peak. On May 7 the governor of Martinique arrived with his wife to calm the residents—Saint-Pierre's total population was about 30,000.

At 8:02 a.m. on May 8, Pelée erupted titanically. A vast burning cloud of gas and steam bearing rocks, lava and ashes roared down the mountainside onto the town. In just three minutes Saint-Pierre was totally wiped out. The only survivor was a prisoner in a thick-walled dungeon who for years afterwards was displayed abroad as a circus attraction. He didn't die until 1955.

The eruption of the volcano is documented in the excellent **Frank Perret museum.** Perret lived in Saint-Pierre from 1929 to 1943. Perched near the crater during the 1929 eruption, he studied the composition of Pelée's volcanic gases, then founded the museum that he donated to the municipality. He died in New York shortly after leaving the island.

French, English and Spanish-speaking guides at the one-room museum help explain the sobering display of relics of the once lively city. Particularly graphic are blown-up old photographs, a burned and twisted sewing machine and a mass of scissors soldered together by the intense heat. One curiosity is a charred electric light fixture and bulb that somehow continued to work for 62 years until it suddenly stopped one day in 1964. The museum is open every day (including Christmas and Carnival) from 9 a.m. to noon and 3 to 5 p.m.

Just outside, glance over the cannon parapet for a view of

Abandoned and overgrown, ruins in St. Pierre testify to tragedy.

Typical of non-resort Martinique, Carbet beach is strictly informal.

the remains of devastated beachside buildings. About 100 yards up the street you'll see the ruins of what was Saint-Pierre's glittering theater and, nearby, the rubble of the old prison.

Today Saint-Pierre is a little town of some 6,500 people. If you ask, natives will probably concede that they always worry a little about "that mountain"

up there, but since the minor eruption in 1929 there has been no smoke and only occasional earth rumblings.

The Far North
History buffs will have to ask along the road north of Saint-Pierre for the unmarked location of the so-called "Caribs'

54

vinelike fig tree and a nice little beach.

The coast here is all but uninhabited. Normally you'll find no one at all on the delightful volcanic sand beach at **Anse Céron.** This idyllic spot is as far as you should attempt to drive —the tropical track ahead will defeat most vehicles.

Instead, to reach Martinique's northernmost villages of Grande-Rivière and Macouba, drive inland from Saint-Pierre, skirting Mount Pelée. This route takes you through LE MORNE ROUGE and AJOUPA BOUILLON. Driving in this region as elsewhere you may be surprised to see brightly painted rubber tires hanging outside houses. These are only for decoration and not intended to ward off "evil spirits"—volcanic or otherwise. For such purposes, some Martiniquais resort to different means.

As you reach the Atlantic coast, you'll become almost engulfed in vast groves of banana trees, with bunches hanging temptingly close to the road. But it's best to steer clear of these groves because they harbor a poisonous snake called the *fer de lance*.

At **Macouba,** it's worth stopping at the simple cliffside church, where Père Labat spent some time, to examine its cem-

Grave," where Indians pursued by French colonists hurled themselves from a cliff in the 17th century, vowing that Mount Pelée would avenge their deaths. Further on is the unassuming village of LE PRÊCHEUR where another island girl who made good spent her childhood years—Madame de Maintenon, second wife of Louis XIV. Beyond Le Prêcheur you'll go through the fishing hamlet of ANSE BELLEVILLE with a remarkably tall,

etery jutting out over the ocean. The lively little fishing settlement far below on the water's edge is an easy walk down, but very tiring coming back up on a hot day. If you do descend, you'll see some rather curious caverns in the limestone cliffs where, on occasion, local people sing and dance to stringed instruments.

Persevering along the bumpy cobblestoned road with its hairpin bends you'll cross two green, modern metal bridges. Then you arrive at **Grande-Rivière.** This end-of-the-road village is famed for its skilled and dauntless fishermen. You'll probably see boys surfing the high, somewhat dangerous Atlantic waves on the smooth trunks of balsa *(langue de bœuf)* trees. This lightweight wood cut to the size of the boy, makes unexpectedly good surfboards.

Saint-Pierre to Fort-de-France

Just off the gray sand **Anse Turin beach** near LE CARBET, a roadside sign reports that Paul Gauguin sojourned here in 1887. The sign points through an arched aqueduct of crumbling stone to the **Musée Gauguin,** displaying some original works by the great French painter, along with a collection of memorabilia (documents, letters, etc.).

Further down the coast road you'll come to Martinique's most-photographed fishing village, **Bellefontaine,** with a beach cluttered with nets and the distinctive *gommier* fishing boats invented by the Carib Indians. Fishing dominates the way of life here, although **Schoelcher,** just north of Fort-de-France, has begun to feel the tourist boom. This expanding town, named after the abolitionist, is proud of its reconstructed Benedictine monastery.

From Fort-de-France, the inland road through the agricultural towns of SAINT-JOSEPH and GROS MORNE meanders over hills thickly planted with bananas, pineapple and sugarcane. You won't envy the men and women you see working in the fields under the blazing sun, but they're never too tired to return your wave with a smile. At Saint-Joseph ask to be shown a "traveler's tree" *(arbre du voyageur)* from Madagascar which has a reserve supply of water within its trunk.

56

Josephine admires the gardens of her birthplace in Martinique.

Much Ado About Josephine

She was certainly not the most attractive of Creole women, but Napoleon didn't set any records for good looks either. Born Marie-Josephe Rose Tascher de la Pagerie on June 23, 1763, she was married at age 16 to Alexandre de Beauharnais, son of Martinique's governor, with whom she had two children and an unhappy life in France. After he was guillotined during the French Revolution, the Creole widow in her thirties met Bonaparte. They were married on March 9, 1796. He called her Josephine and clearly adored her. When he took power and forged his empire, she was made his empress. FWI gossips say she had many lovers, fascinating men with her "interesting character." Josephine might have ruled until the end, but when by 1809 she had produced no son, Napoleon divorced her. She died five years later in France, revered to this day in her native Martinique.

South Along the Caribbean

By any standards **Trois Ilets** seems an unlikely hometown for an empress. The village is named after the three small islands it overlooks in a corner of Fort-de-France's huge bay. Don't miss the neatly whitewashed church with a pale blue 57 ceiling above its cool interior. Here Josephine's parents were married and she was baptized, though the plaque notes merely that the village celebrated the 100th anniversary of Napoleon's death on May 5, 1921.

About five minutes away in the unspoiled countryside, you'll jolt over the 200 rockiest yards of road in Martinique to get to the **Musée de la Pagerie.** Contained in the restored kitchen and prayer room of Josephine's family estate, the tidy little museum is a shrine to the one-time empress. You'll see period furniture, slave chains and old paintings, but the greatest attractions are a photocopy of Napoleon and Josephine's wedding certificate and an emotional love letter he wrote her in 1796 from Italy (an English translation is displayed). Guides who speak some English as well as French and Creole will shyly tell you that visitors to this out-of-the-way memorial have included

Queen Margrethe of Denmark, King Leopold of Belgium, Lady Clementine Churchill and Jacqueline Kennedy Onassis.

Just down the road from the museum lie the rolling fairways of Martinique's 18-hole golf course and a little further on, the **Pointe du Bout** resort with its cluster of hotels, beaches and a marina. If you continue by boat around this most attractive peninsula, you'll notice several secluded little coves scooped out of the often steep coastline. By car or ferry from Fort-de-France, you can reach **Anse à l'Ane** which has a pleasant brown-sand beach with sea grapes providing shade, picnic tables, children's slides and restaurants. There's also an un-

Diamond Rock is a 2-mile swim; Pointe du Bout an effortless ferry ride.

usual seashell museum here (*Musée d'Art en Coquillage*) with intricately constructed tableaus of local and historical scenes. Open daily except Tuesday.

Even better is **Les Anses-d'Arlets,** as delightful a village as there is anywhere in the French West Indies. You may have to share the three fine little beaches with a few cheerful fishermen. The Caribbean here is usually placid, always inviting. And the atmosphere is utterly relaxed, the tiny village quiet and clean. Motorboats from the capital will bring you out here in record time.

After a stop to contemplate Diamond Rock (see box), most tourists continue south over winding roads through SAINTE-LUCE, RIVIÈRE-PILOTE and LE MARIN without stopping until they reach SAINTE-ANNE. The best beach, perhaps the best on the entire island, is nearby within the confines of a private vacation club. It runs along into a perfectly acceptable public beach which has, unfortunately, very little shade. (Though the equator is only a mite closer here in the rather arid south of Martinique, the sun does seem measurably hotter than elsewhere on the island.)

Having reached Sainte-Anne, you should certainly drive south for perhaps ten minutes, as far as the road permits, to the string of beautiful, deserted beaches known as **Les Salines.** Take your lunch; this is wild, far-out Caribbean beach territory with no facilities of any kind although some islanders keep tents here permanently for weekend camping. The area is named after the large salt pond you'll see.

This is also the site of a

Diamond Rock
(*Le Rocher du Diamant*)
Jutting up from the sea some 2 miles off-shore, its massive bulk covered with green shrubs, it doesn't at all resemble a British battleship. In fact, it is the only rock commissioned as a sloop of war in the Royal Navy. During the bitter struggle for Martinique, the British landed a contingent of men and supplies on H.M.S. *Diamond Rock* in 1804. It took the French 18 months of bombardment and assaults to dislodge the garrison and thus regain control of the sea channel between the rock and the coast.

Military exigencies long past, birds have the strange, looming rock to themselves nowadays.

strange "petrified savanna forest" *(la savanne des pétrifications)*, rather difficult to reach over rutted automobile trails of rock and sand. Here, as far south as you can go on Martinique, the landscape is desolate. Only cacti seem able to grow amid bleak rocks that on inspection turn out to be petrified wood. It's speculated that aeons ago this may have been a forest extinguished by the eruption of some volcano now deep under the sea.

All kinds of beautiful items turn up on the FWI's smiling beaches.

The Atlantic Coast

Though at points very attractive, the windward coast of Martinique is not of great tourist interest. Much of this rugged shoreline is accessible only by boat. The only worthwhile beach area is near TARTANE on the mid-island **Caravelle peninsula** where there's also a park with walking trails.

You'll enjoy visiting **Le Vauclin,** a consummate fishing village with more than its share of friendly, weatherbeaten people. Much evidence of a major Carib Indian settlement has been unearthed in this region. The spectacular views of the whole of southern Martinique from Mount Vauclin are noteworthy.

Further up the coast, LE FRANÇOIS is a curious blend of typical wooden homes and brashly modern apartment buildings spreading down toward a pretty bay where there's a lazy marina.

Saint-Martin

It's an island with a dual personality—each side trying to outsmile the other. Whatever you call it, Saint-Martin, as the French do, or Sint Maarten with the Dutch, it is part of both the French West Indies and the Netherlands' Antilles.

Columbus named the island after St. Martin on that saint's feast day in 1493—or did he? Given the inexact state of the

On a St. Martin vacation; if not on the water, you'll be near it.

geography along the confusing Antilles chain, some experts suggest that he actually gave the name to Nevis, an island to the south, and that subsequent cartographers somehow awarded it to Saint-Martin. The similarity to Matinino–Martinique—only confuses things more.

63

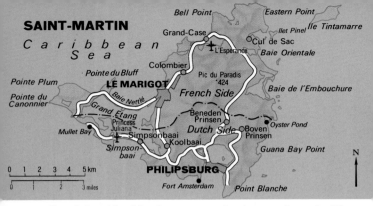

Certainly this island can qualify as having one of the world's longest-running governmental love affairs: since 1648 the French and the Dutch have shared sovereignty in almost total harmony. When the two nations divided it up, France got 21 square miles and Holland agreed to take just 16, but that included the important salt pond near the Dutch capital of Philipsburg.*

Another thing those early French and Dutch settlers agreed upon was that their island should be free of levies on any imported goods. That still means completely duty-free shopping today and therefore —together with nearby Saint-Barthélemy— the Caribbean's lowest prices for many items (see pp. 84–86).

Theoretically, there is a frontier, but there isn't a single customs official and it's been unguarded for over 300 years. On the main highway you'll know you've passed it by a stone monument commemorating the partition and signs reading *Bienvenue Partie Française* in one direction, "Welcome to Sint Maarten" in the other—that's all. Since the island's telephone service can be some what capricious, it's often easier to drive across the border than to put through a call to the other side. So near, yet worlds apart, the two sides

---

* Legend has it that the division was accomplished by having a Frenchman and a Dutchman start back to back pacing off territory: some say the Frenchman got more of the island because he had a longer stride—or that the Dutchman stopped too often for a snort of gin.

maintain their separate identities: the Dutch side, despite such hold-outs as thin cigars, gin and Indonesian *rijsttafel,* has begun to resemble an American beachhead after years of landings by hordes of cruise ship shoppers.

On the French side of the island—a sub-prefecture of Guadeloupe—every schoolchild learns the mother tongue. There is a Creole patois, heavily influenced by immigrants from Haiti, but it's essentially based on French. Here, on the northernmost of the FWI, you'll find such familiar trappings as *boulangeries,* restaurants featuring delicate wine sauces and gendarmes (if only a mere handful). Around 10,000 people live on the French side, about 20,000 on the Dutch.

Marigot

Whereas Dutch Sint Maarten is one of the more upbeat places in the Caribbean, much of the French side's charm is that it seems content to slumber languidly in the sun. Marigot, the modest capital on its wide bay, is so quiet that very large fish venture in surprisingly close to shore. You'll also see plenty of yachts, but cruise ships don't call—Philipsburg gets them all.

When Marigot does liven up—early in the day at the quayside—you'll want to be there. Like their Guadeloupean and Martiniquais counterparts, Saint-Martin's fishermen invariably chug home with their catches to a clamorous welcome. Nearby, ladies with broad smiles—and beams—sit on little stools selling breadfruit and cinnamon. Things become almost chaotic, by Marigot standards, when an inter-island cargo scow arrives with haphazardly tethered livestock and straw-hatted voyagers.

The Dutch have a fort, so the French have a fort. For the view over Marigot Bay, it's worth the four-minute climb up to deserted old **Fort Saint-Louis.** This 17th-century bastion looks its age and then some. Sheep graze alongside a rusty, disused cannon—standard armament of FWI forts.

A few minutes up and over the hill by car is **Grand-Case,** a delightful village strung unpretentiously along a long, curving beach. Much smaller than Marigot and even lower-keyed, it has several restaurants and places to stay. At salt flats nearby is tiny Espérance airport, a one-strip, one-shed affair used for flights to and from Pointe-à-Pitre and Saint-Barthélemy.

The Beaches and the Sea

Counting little coves you'll reach only by boat, Saint-Martin has 36 beaches of fine, sometimes dazzling white sand with hotels located on some of the best. Following the avant-garde lead of big sister Guadeloupe, Saint-Martin has introduced a nudist beach.

Surfy or serene, deep blue or aquamarine, the water is clear and clean. Snorkeling and skin diving are particularly rewarding at a number of isolated inlets and nearby islets, and boats to take you there are available. The 1801 wreck of a British warship on a reef three miles offshore is a diver's dream; for the non-scuba set there's a glass-bottomed boat you can take to see big groupers and perhaps sea turtles swimming around the sunken ships' cannons.

Sailboats of various sizes are offered for rent around the island. Beginners appreciate the calm waters of Simson Bay, the largest lagoon in the West Indies. Old salts may want to skipper their charter craft across open sea to the smaller Dutch islands of Sint Eustatius or Saba, or to French Saint-Barthélemy. If you don't "do-it-yourself," there's a choice of one-day group excursions by motor launch or sailboat. Hotels will be able to arrange for deep-sea fishing and water-skiing.

Exotic blooms and foliage flourish in the year-round blissful climate. Unspoilt coast of St. Martin.

Touring the Island

Without seriously disrupting the leisurely pace of your vacation, you can see the highlights of Saint-Martin in one day, breaking for a swim and a relaxed lunch. There's a great deal of pastureland with stone walls. And not a traffic jam on the island. Rental car firms offer descriptive tape cassettes for your own guided tour. Otherwise, agencies run bus tours and taxi drivers are pleased to drive you around.

Today's coconut may be tomorrow's soup, ice-cream or cocktail.

Probably the most exciting things to see on the island are other islands. Outside Philipsburg from a roadside lookout point you'll make out four islands rising out of the sea in the distance: Nevis, St. Kitts, Sint Eustatius and Saba. More dramatically, from the high, serpentine road to Oyster Pond from Philipsburg, you'll be stunned by the beauty of Saint-Barthélemy across a royal blue swath of the Atlantic.

SAINT-BARTHELEMY

🎒 Saint-Barthélemy

This just might be the best piece of France anywhere. Known fondly as "St. Barts"—Columbus bestowed his brother's name, Bartholomew, on the island when he sailed past in 1493—it's an absolutely peaceful, absolutely beautiful little island of roller coaster hills, rocky coves and powdery beaches lining a limpid, emerald sea.

Twittering in the shrubbery of its 8 square miles are countless thousands of yellow breasts, red throats and hummingbirds. They greatly outnumber the 3,000-odd inhabitants—mostly white, many the descendants of Huguenots from Brittany and Normandy.

These unusual Frenchmen and the relative handful of black families that have also lived here for generations strike visitors as extremely kind, open and simple. Among themselves they speak a nasal, old-fashioned French, accented in a way that reminds visiting Parisians of French-Canadian speech. Sprinkled through it are bits of English and Swedish.* The result is a patois baffling to anyone not brought up on St. Barts.

Now that he island has a modern international airport, people are making their way to St. Barts in ever-increasing numbers. Swelling the ranks of American vacationers are trendy young Frenchmen from the *métropole*. They like

---

* For nearly a century, until 1878, St. Barts was the only possession Sweden ever had in the Western hemisphere (see p. 22).

the relaxed, low-key atmosphere and Gallic flair of the place. The tourist influx has triggered a building boom around the island and in the tiny capital of Gustavia, situated on a picture-postcard harbor. Some new hotels have opened, but so far, St. Barts has lost none if its former charm.

The most popular way to get there is by scheduled flight from Saint-Martin or Guadeloupe. Unless you arrive by yacht, the other option is a motor-launch ride from Saint-Martin, 15—sometimes very choppy—nautical miles away.

Gustavia

When you see it, you'll understand why Gustavia's rectangular harbor is a favorite with the Caribbean yachting set. From this ideal anchorage you can rent small excursion or fishing boats. *Caution:* Owing to the risk of *ciguatera* in the Caribbean (see p. 115), you'd be wise to check with local experts before eating any fish you catch in offshore waters.

In one morning you can get to know just about everybody in this unassuming island capital. The Swedes named it after King Gustav III and, in 1785, declared it the free port that it remains today. Shopping is

therefore duty-free, as in Saint-Martin (see p. 84). Liquor and tobacco are good buys. There are also several French boutiques that stock merchandise from the Continent, though the selection of items for sale is rather limited.

When sight-seeing, you'll find the two thriving churches somewhat more interesting than the three ruined forts overlooking Gustavia. St. Barts, of course, is completely undefended. But then this very particular island is hardly in danger of being invaded—except, of course, by tourism.

Around the Island

Sightseers have their choice of taxi or rental vehicles, including the ubiquitous mini-moke and beach buggy ideal for local conditions. To spend more than four hours covering every paved and unpaved road, most of which terminate in unannounced dead ends, would be a difficult task. If you're stranded anywhere, hitch-hiking is accepted behavior and you'll surely get a ride. In recent years, the number of motor vehicles on St. Barts has escalated to something like two per inhabitant.

The seascapes and panoramas on this island are enough

to tempt any driver to glance away from the serviceable, but never-wide-enough roads. From the highest point on the **Vitet road,** you'll want to stop to take in the sweeping view over a bay called Grand Cul-de-Sac, which is favored by windsurfers, and out to Tortue islet in the Atlantic. Not far away is **Pointe Milou,** a wild, breathtaking headland from which on a clear day you can count nine isles or rocks in the

At famous Saint-Jean beach, the surf is gentle, the tempo sleepy.

sea. The strange cactus-like plants growing here in great profusion are called *Tête à l'Anglais.* They have prominent red protuberances and may have been named after the British redcoats.

The French West Indies may be matriarchal, but on St. Barts the father runs the family. Practically everyone goes to church, the Catholic majority either on Saturday evening or Sunday when mass is celebrated at different churches. It's worth going to church or visiting the fishing hamlet of COROSSOL just to see the ladies wearing the starched white bonnets called *quichenottes,* a St. Barts' trademark that dates back to the time of the original Huguenot settlers.

Beaches

The very best are difficult to get to, as is often the case with superior beaches in the Caribbean. Coconut trees and sloping cliffs ring the tranquil waters of **Colombier.** This northern beach of magnificent tan sand is most agreeably reached by boat. Otherwise when the road gives out, you'll have to walk for about half an hour to this paradise bay which a noted American banker, David Rockefeller, chose as the site of his Caribbean vacation home. Members of the Rothschild and Ford families have also taken up residence in the area.

Very bumpy roads will take you almost as far as the second- and third-best beaches, **Gouverneur** and **Grande Saline,** in neighboring coves on the south coast. Sea grapes and shrubs provide little shade here, but otherwise you should find no fault with either of these beaches. Legend has it that treasure lies buried somewhere hereabouts, hidden away by a renowned French buccaneer called Montbars the Exterminator.

There's no access problem to **Saint-Jean,** the best known and most-photographed of Saint-Barthélemy's 22 beaches. There are actually two shimmering crescents of pale sand here, separated by a small rocky promontory.

At **Corossol, Anse des Cayes** and **Anse de Lorient,** you'll share the shore with fishermen, who set out to sea in gaily painted boats.

Currents can be surprisingly strong at the attractive **Flamands beach**—not recommended for children or poor swimmers. At many points around St. Barts and its small rocky offshore islets, there is fine reef snorkeling.

What to Do

Sports

Regardless of the time of year you visit these islands, you'll spend most of your time outdoors on or near the water—and a word of caution is necessary. The rays of the tropical sun here can cause you serious trouble. In no more than 15 to 20 minutes, fair skin can be painfully broiled, *even* in the shade of a coconut tree. For the first few days you'd be well advised to take the sun in extremely small doses.

Swimming

Coral or volcanic, eggshell white or ashy gray, the sand of FWI beaches varies from cove to cove. Your hotel may be on an outstanding beach. If not, there's usually one within easy reach. In Guadeloupe, the best white or brown sand beaches are on Grande-Terre, as are most of the hotels. Basse-Terre features both dark volcanic sand in the region of Mount Soufrière and beige beaches in the north. Local lore says that you tan better on black sand.

Martinique's Mount Pelée provides the dark coloring for it's northern beaches. Saint-Martin and Saint-Barthélemy, though also volcanic in formation, but without erupting peaks, have only light sand beaches.

Swimming conditions vary enormously on all the islands. You'll have no trouble in identifying the many perfectly safe, protected shores where hardly a ripple disturbs the surface. Otherwise, there are some beaches or sections of beaches where swimming is less recommended or even dangerous for all except experts. Coral reefs often reduce wave strength but may not stem very strong ocean currents, particularly in the Atlantic. Time of year is also a factor, the winter months bringing heavier seas. On Martinique the Tourist Office advises that the safest beaches for poor swimmers are at Sainte-Anne, Trois-Ilets, Sainte-Luce, Trinité and Carbet.

Good tidings about the shark situation: no incident involving a swimmer, snorkeler or diver has been reported anywhere in the FWI. Guadeloupe, incredibly, almost never sees a shark anywhere near its coast. Sightings close to Martinique are very rare and not much more frequent off the northern FWI. Nonetheless, swimming after dusk is not advisable. **73**

For a small fee, non-guests may use the beach and facilities at a number of Guadeloupe and Martinique hotels—a great convenience for island hoppers. Alternatively, there are also fine public beaches—and they're often deserted.

Many hotels have swimming pools, for those allergic to sand.

Snorkeling, Skin Diving, Scuba Diving

Underwater sports off the major islands and rocky islets of the FWI are the highlights of countless vacations. Snorkeling equipment may be provided free, rented or bought inexpensively in tourist areas, so there's no need to bring any from home. Beginners who can stay afloat can learn to breathe through the tube and peer through the mask in minutes.

Many of the best snorkeling and underwater photography areas are offshore—at coral reefs or around uninhabited islands; you'll have little difficulty in finding a boat to take you out. Such multicolored reef dwellers as the parrotfish and French angelfish, along with weirdly shaped coral, crawfish or turtles hiding in crevices, can be yours for the

viewing in these clear waters where visibility of 100 feet is common.

Free-dive spear fishing (without air container) is permitted in the FWI, but always check with local fishermen before eating anything you catch (see HEALTH p. 115). You should see many of the following: grouper, amberjack, red or rock hind, stingrays, Atlantic rays and moray eels. Equipment may be rented at watersports establishments.

Scuba (an acronym for Self-Contained Underwater Breathing Apparatus) is taught and offered at major hotels. This ultimate subsurface experience is becoming very popular in France, as it has been for a number of years in the United States. The Caribbean's transparency and teeming underwater life make it ideal for scuba, and since the water stays tropically warm year-round, you shouldn't need a full wet suit.

Boating, Windsurfing and Water-Skiing

A large number of hotels in the FWI have small boats available for rent, including the always popular Sunfish. You can also find instructors able to give sailing lessons, as well as all kinds of boat excursions on which a skipper and crew do the work while you relax.

Windsurfing is making a splash in the FWI: you'll see **75**

the colorful sails, boards and masts all around the islands. It looks easier than it is—you'll need lessons, at least two or three just to get you started.

Water skiing is somewhat harder to find, but certain hotels do provide motorboats and skis with fixed rates for a 10-minute *tour* and an additional fee per lesson. The more *tours* you buy, the lower the rate, so water-ski enthusiasts will certainly get value for money.

Sailing and Yachting

With balmy trade winds, infrequent squalls and flowing sea currents, the FWI and nearby Antilles are ideal for a day, a week or a month under sail. As every islander knows, many of the most gorgeous coves and beaches are reachable only by boat. For a fairly modest sum per person, you might consider chartering a skippered sloop or catamaran for a full day.

From Martinique, the popular 10-day or two-week sail takes you to St. Lucia and

Windsurfing—a fashionable sport that looks like staying in the FWI's **77**

down into the Grenadines. From Guadeloupe, try Les Saintes and Marie-Galante, which both have safe anchorages or sail further to Antigua. A 40-foot two-masted vessel sleeping a maximum of six with captain and one crew member can be taken from either Martinique or Guadeloupe—for a small fortune, of course.

To do it yourself, or charter "bareboat," you'll need to demonstrate proficiency. You'll find various vessels for charter at the yachting *carénage* in Pointe-à-Pitre, at Fort-de-France or across its bay at the Pointe du Bout marina, and at Marigot. During the peak season (mid-December to mid-April) rates are higher.

Among the yachts advertised for charter in Guadeloupe is an 80-foot ketch built for the late King Farouk.

Fishing

The FWI are somewhat removed from the great game-fishing waters off the Bahamas, Puerto Rico and the Virgin Islands, but the average angler will find challenges aplenty here from boat or shore. There are a limited number of deep-sea boats for charter; they normally accommodate up to four persons. Local fishermen will also cheerfully take you out in their time-tested, no-frills boats. This may mean you'll have to help with nets or traps, an instructive experience.

Surf casting with lures (called *spinning*), is outstanding at three points in southeast Martinique—Cap Ferré, Cap Macré and Cap Chevalier. Local buffs say it's also excellent at Ilet Hardy, Pointe Baham and Grande-Rivière. Expect to haul in jacks, barracuda, yellowtail snapper, tarpon (best with bait off Vauclin), dolphin, red hind and jewfish.

Bottom fishing may get you grouper, tarpon, mahogany or red snapper, parrotfish, grunts and, rarely, African pompano. In Martinique the best bottom fishing is probably at Robert and Les Salines.

Guadeloupe, with more fully equipped ocean-going boats than Martinique, offers deep-sea fishing for kingfish, tuna, barracuda, bonito and dolphin. You should find some or all of these in Saint-Martin's waters as well, with about a dozen boats available for charter. Wahoo, one of the "big five" game fish, is hooked occasionally off all the islands.

Before frying up your catch, remember to check with local fishermen about edibility (see HEALTH, p. 115).

Golf

A few long fairway shots away from Josephine's birthplace at La Pagerie is Martinique's 18-hole public golf course. It's also only a short ride (1 ½ miles) from the Pointe du Bout hotels, some of which have special package arrangements with the club. The prolific American golfing architect Robert Trent Jones designed this rolling 6,640-yard course, a factor ensuring that it's not easy to play. It's generally windy here, and there are eight water holes (including two on the Fort-de-France bay).

Guadeloupe's 18-hole course, also a creation of Robert Trent

Blood Sports

The French islands enthusiastically share the West Indian passion for cockfighting. Two specially trained cocks, steel spurs attached to their feet, battle until one is killed in a so-called *pitt* while spectators, who bet large sums on the outcome, cheer the combatants. Anyone can tell you where to find a cockfight.

You may also run across mongoose-snake fights on the islands. Normally the mongoose, or a replacement if the original falters, kills the snake.

France and Tennis Club du Vieux Moulin—when the courts are not in use). Playing away from your hotel could be very expensive during the day and exorbitant under lights. Rackets may be rented. Surfaces are artificial. Professionals give lessons at many hotels, the price sometimes included in tennis-package vacations. Until you're accustomed to the climate, play only before 10 in the morning and in the late afternoon and evening.

Jones, is near Saint-François on Grande-Terre.

Greens fees depend on which hotel you are staying at. Material for hire includes electric cars and pull carts. Or you can engage a caddy; it's always pleasant to have company.

On Saint-Martin tourists may use the Mullet Bay 18-hole course on the Dutch side.

Tennis

You'll be able to play tennis by day or night at all of Guadeloupe's resort hotels, at most of Saint-Martin's and at some of Martinique's (where tourists may also use two private clubs —Tennis Club de Fort-de-

Horseback Riding

There are several stables on Martinique where hotels can arrange for tourists to rent horses by the hour or the day. Or you can join an organized group excursion following country trails through scenic landscapes.

On Guadeloupe rides in the countryside can be arranged. For further information contact Comité Guadeloupéen des Sports Equestres, B.P. 758, 97172 Pointe-à-Pitre.

On St. Barts "La Petite Ferme" organizes rides on Sundays.

Leafy path leads to Guadeloupe's Carbet falls—a rewarding walk.

Hiking

Guadeloupe's huge Natural Park has trails laid out through the tropical forest, up to major waterfalls and on to the crater of Mount Soufrière. You'll find a printed guide indicating times and difficulty of various hikes at the Pointe-à-Pitre tourist office.

On Martinique, trails have been marked through the Caravelle peninsula nature reserve, and local guides will take you along more rugged trails around Mount Pelée in the north. A hiking path connects Le Prêcheur with Grande-Rivière, advertised as a six-hour journey.

Shopping

If you're not French, think French. Particularly on Martinique and Guadeloupe where the outstanding bargains are in perfumes, Parisian fashions, crystal and other luxury items from France. On duty-free Saint-Martin and Saint-Barthélemy, the range of best buys is even greater. There are local handicraft items for sale on all four islands that are interesting and reasonably priced, but shop around off the obvious tourist

However humble a shop may appear, its variety could be surprising.

beat and don't hesitate to bargain.

At hotel boutiques, prices may or may not be the same as in urban shopping areas: for anything major, it's worth comparing. Opening hours are as follows: ordinary shops and stores 8 a.m. to noon and 2 to 5 p.m.; supermarkets, department stores and bookshops 8:30 a.m. to 12:30 p.m. and 2:30 to 5:30 p.m.; boutiques 9 a.m. to 1 p.m. and 3 to 6 p.m.

Some stores are open after normal hours or on Sundays or holidays when cruise ships are in port. Better shops are air-conditioned.

All of the islands accept American or Canadian dollars about as readily as French francs. Many shops in Guadeloupe and Martinique give discounts (usually 20 per cent) for purchases in traveler's checks, but not normally if you pay in foreign currency. On Martinique you're likely to get the same discount if you pay with one of the major credit cards.

Neither Martinique nor Guadeloupe enjoy duty-free status (apart from the duty-free shops at the airports), but almost everything from France is sold at mainland French prices, well below what the items would cost in North America.

While Americans returning home must pay duty on everything above $300 worth of purchases made abroad, the US customs levy added to the price of an item may still come to less than what it would cost in Boston or Chicago.

A wise idea is to price major items at home before your vacation.

To avoid possible complications with customs, veteran travelers ask for and retain a receipt (sales slip) for everything purchased.

Guadeloupe's Shopping Scene

Aside from a few boutiques and native crafts shops around the island, notably in or near hotels, interesting shopping is concentrated in an area of Pointe-à-Pitre several city blocks square, beginning at the cruise ship dock.

Best buys: French perfumes, silk items, porcelain, crystal, liqueurs and vintage wines.

Good buys: cloth hangings of Creole scenes, seashell jewelry, straw mats and hats particularly from Saint-Barthélemy, local rum and conch shells (beautiful specimens can be had for just a few francs **83**

apiece from curbside peddlers near the maritime terminal, but only when a cruise ship is about to depart).

A standard Guadeloupe souvenir is a puffed-up, porcupine-spined puffer fish *(poisson lune)* which, if large enough, can become an offbeat lampshade. You should also see items crafted from shark's teeth and occasionally even entire jaws.

Martinique's Shopping Scene

Much of downtown Fort-de-France is fertile territory for shoppers. For tourists at Pointe du Bout, it's worth taking the 20-minute ferry ride to the capital to investigate prices there before shopping at the resort hotel boutiques. Elsewhere on the island there are a handful of craft workshops.

Best buys: perfumes and other French luxury items as listed for Guadeloupe; you'll also find neckties and the best Parisian silk scarves on sale at reasonable prices (which incorporates a 20 per cent traveler's check discount).

Good buys: the island's typical *poupée martiniquaise,* a doll in Creole madras costume on sale everywhere; tapestries, **84** wicker trays and boxes and

Goods may not all be handmade, but in this setting, who cares?

the memorable dark (aged) or white rum.

Before buying anthuriums or other flowers, check your re-entry regulations at home.

Facing the ferry pier on the Fort-de-France waterfront is an outdoor pavilion where you might try bargaining for straw hats and baskets, conch shells, huge wooden forks or seashell necklaces. Some of the salesladies at this colorful, soft-sell market wear traditional Martinique costumes. Fort-de-France's main shopping streets, tourist-oriented or not, are between the Savane and the Levassor River.

Shops on Martinique stock a selection of mainland Chinese, Philippine, African, Haitian and Japanese jewelry. Watch for onyx from Argentina and shark-cartilage pendants from Uruguay, among other exotic items.

Duty-Free Delights: Saint-Martin and Saint-Barthélemy

For most items, the two small northern FWI have the lowest prices in the Caribbean. Some

Despite the time and care devoted to basket-making, prices are low.

residents of the "duty-free" U.S. Virgin Islands nearby even do their Christmas shopping in Philipsburg, Marigot or Gustavia. It takes a while to realize that not just certain stores, but *every* store on these islands sells at the same taxless, duty-free prices.

Almost everything is quoted in U.S. dollars, but, of course, you can pay in French francs or Netherlands Antilles guilders. While prices for French perfumes and fashions may not be appreciably lower here than in the rest of the FWI, they could be half of what Americans would pay at home.

In all three little capitals, shopping begins where the boats come in. There are also a few small shops in Grand Case.

Best buys on French Saint-Martin and to a lesser extent on St. Barts include: perfumes and cosmetics, luggage, fashions, fabrics including madras, crystal, leather, figurines and children's clothes.

At the busy Front Street shops in Philipsburg, the "lowest tobacco prices in the Caribbean" include a selection of Cuban cigars. Other best buys here: watches, radios, binoculars, tape recorders, some cameras, Delft blue, jewels, Thai silks, linens, Peruvian mirrors, old silver and liquor.

Not everything is automatically a bargain: American tourists may find that certain calculators and cameras, for example, are just as inexpensive at discount stores back home. However, on Saint-Martin and St. Barts you'll also be saving the city or state sales tax that may be levied at home.

Local Culture and Events

Music and Dance

Swaying rhythms are among the most appealing aspects of life in the French West Indies. While islanders of all ages love to dance, you may have to search a bit nowadays to find the gay and flirtatious *biguine,* the romantic Creole mazurka or *mazouk,* the sensually suggestive *calenda.* Like the rest of the Caribbean, the FWI are inundated by the marvelous steel band *calypsos* of Trinidad, the *merengue* of Dominica, the *reggae* and *rampa*—not to

Martiniquais clapping and singing encourages impromptu drum concert.

mention North American and European pop music, courtesy of the transistor.

The authentic FWI dances originated with the African slaves. Some are adaptations of those of the French plantation masters. The *biguine,* immortalized for Anglo-Saxons by Cole Porter, is thought to have come first to Martinique from the Congo. Those Creole men and women you'll see dancing it properly have been moving their hips and knees that way since childhood. Dixieland fans will notice the instrumental similarity to New Orleans—banjo, clarinet, bass, trombone and drums.

The *laghia* in which two men, dancing to drums alone, simulate a fierce kicking combat, arrived with slaves from Dahomey. Only in the country during patron saint day festivals or at a folk dance performance are you likely to see *le rose,* a slave woman's washing dance; *grage,* with dancers mimicking tapioca graters to the beat of goatskin drums; the *haute-taille,* an adaptation with accordion and drums of a European quadrille; or the *bel-air,* an African-Creole version of a three-figure quadrille.

Twenty-five young dancers, singers and musicians in the Ballets Martiniquais Folklore group perform traditional local favorites, as do less formal groups on Guadeloupe. Here you'll see the delightful but slowly disappearing indigenous FWI costume—madras turban, madras skirt over petticoat, silk peplum, white blouse and gold earrings, bracelets and *collier-choux* necklace.

Carnival

It may not be the wildest in the Caribbean, but the FWI's carnival *is* the longest, by 24 hours. Early in the week there are pajama, "doudou" doll and pirate parades plus always-spectacular carnival floats. The riotous revelry roars right past Mardi Gras (Shrove Tuesday) when red-costumed children star as devils, to its peak on Ash Wednesday. Downtown Fort-de-France and Pointe-à-Pitre are flooded with dancers, notably *diablesses,* all dressed

Ballets Martiniquais performers have as much fun as the audience.

in black and white and losing themselves in the *biguine*. The carnival king, Vaval, is burned in effigy after dusk, but the frenzied dancing goes on till after midnight.

Special Events

Aside from carnival and patron saints' days in the towns, you'll enjoy:

Fishermen's Festival *(Fête des Marins Pêcheurs)* late in June on Martinique, with parades, fish feasts and traditional costumes.

Cooks' Festival *(Fête des Cuisiniers)* in early August in Pointe-à-Pitre, with a colorful, appetite-stimulating parade, a religious ceremony honoring Saint Laurent (chosen as the local cooks' patron saint because in A.D. 258 he was burned alive on a rack, which is now a kitchen utensil) and a monumental free feast with singing, dancing and liberal applications of rum punch.

All Saints' Day *(La Toussaint)* November 1, when, after dark, in an original and beautiful Antilles tradition, all graves in cemeteries are illuminated with candles.

All the fun of the fair; FWI dancers whirl wildly through the night.

Folk Beliefs

Don't sleep in the rays of the moon—your facial features will be distorted. Pour some rum into a dead man's mouth to cheer him up, otherwise he'll come back to haunt the house. These and other superstitions are held by many FWI citizens. Many of the strange twigs, herbs and packets you'll see in the markets have to do with magic based on traditions that stem from the African origins of most of the population. This is not, however, the voodoo of Haiti, and there are no "black magic" performances staged for tourists.

Early missionaries used to say *tiens, bois!* (here, drink!) when they gave medicine to ailing islanders. It seemed magical when maladies were cured, and from *tiens, bois* derived the word *quimbois,* for magic potion or spell. Today in most villages on Martinique and Guadeloupe there are still *quimboiseurs* who mix the mysterious concoctions. They are considered useful for divining the future, prescribing remedies for problems and perhaps putting a spell on an enemy.

The ordinary tourist will find it difficult to obtain precise details about this magic, which is known as *obeah* around the West Indies.

Nightlife

There's little danger that the French West Indies will ever be overrun with "swinging" after-hours resorts. But Guadeloupe is making an effort. On its "riviera" along the southern coast of Grand-Terre, in addition to hotel lounges there are a number of private discotheques and rural nightclubs. Tourists are welcome at such nightspots, where they're likely to be outnumbered by rhythm-loving Guadeloupeans. Advertisements suggest there is striptease occasionally in this area, logical—or illogical?—on an island promoting nudism.

On Martinique, all but the most adventurous tourists will prefer dancing and drinking in their hotels. Here they'll have the latest calypso mixed with more familiar pop and soul. The admission charge at hotel lounges includes the first drink. Fort-de-France and its suburbs have a smattering of very local, very crowded discotheques where foreigners rarely appear. One reason: most of the island's resort hotels are quite a distance from the capital.

If folklore performers, steel bands or limbo dancers visit your resort area, they usually perform during dinner, so you just sit down and enjoy the show—usually outdoors.

Guadeloupe and Martinique have a couple of hotel casinos, modest and low-keyed by international standards, but perfectly able to accommodate you if you'd like to risk your next year's salary. The casinos, open nightly from 9 p.m. until at least 3 a.m., offer roulette,

American blackjack, baccarat and sometimes craps and, in Martinique, French *boule*. Drinks are available—and expensive.

There's an admission charge (less in Martinique than in Guadeloupe), you must be at least 21, and *each time* you go, you must present your passport or other official identification. At a slightly disadvantageous rate, you can exchange foreign currency or traveler's checks for franc chips. Succumbing to Caribbean-wide informality, the casinos do not require men to wear a tie or jacket.

If your French is good or just needs some polishing, both major islands have movie theaters that show European and American films with French soundtracks only. Seat prices won't ruin you.

On Saint-Martin, lingering over a seaside dinner is the preferred after-dark activity on the French side, where most lights go out by 9 or 10 p.m. For livelier late-nights spots, head for the Dutch side with its revues and well-publicized hotel casinos.

On St. Barts, soon after nightfall, the most popular leisure activity is sleep. It may sound dull, but on an island like this, just think of the dreams!

Guadeloupe limbo dancer keeps his cool in this warming performance.

93

Wining and Dining

Just as you'd expect, the French islands offer the best eating in the Caribbean. Surprising perhaps is that it's the piquant Creole dishes as much as the imported staples of French cuisine that make dining such a treat. Your gourmet chef might be a native of Lyons, or a simple village in the Guadeloupean hinterland. Either way, 4,000 odd miles from Paris, you'll notice that extra effort, the touch of flair characteristic of a nation that cherishes good food above almost all else.

North American visitors are thrilled to find real *croissants,* non-plastic Camemberts, those incomparable crusty loaves of French white bread *(baguettes)* and château wines. All four islands have a number of French restaurants, their menus straight out of continental France. There may, of course, be a difference in quality, since almost everything must be imported: your veal in mushroom sauce or duck with orange had a long and probably frozen journey.

But there's also every good reason to sample the recipes with local ingredients perfected by island chefs. Creole restaurants abound, and most are smaller, less elaborate and less expensive than the hotel dining rooms.

Restaurants serve lunch from 12:30 until 2:30 or 3 p.m.; dinner from 7.30 to 9 p.m. Dining is often outdoors, never formal; but it's best to have your concierge book a table at popular restaurants. Usually a service charge (of up to 15 per cent) is added onto your check.

So, doing as the French West Indians do, after your *ti rhum*

Buffet lunch with inevitably tropical touch is a standard hotel feature.

punch (little rum punch), you'll have some or all of these to choose from:

Appetizers or First Courses
Accras—typical Creole fritters (croquettes, French *beignets*), stuffed with salt codfish, sea urchins, shrimp, meat or vegetables; served hot and eaten with the fingers. *Accras à pis-*

quettes, stuffed with a tiny, transparent local fish, has been called the triumph of Guadeloupean gastronomy.

Harengs fumés à la Créole—smoked herring (usually Norwegian) flamed in rum, served with a sauce of hot pepper, vinegar, oil and onion, accompanied by the excellent FWI cucumbers or avocados. **95**

Boudin noir—spicy black pudding (blood sausage).

Potage à la crème de coco—cream of coconut soup, served hot, perhaps in the husk itself.

Pâté en pot—normally mutton soup with vegetables, wine, capers and cognac; occasionally including chopped turtle meat *(pâté en pot tortue)*.

Soupe z'habitant—a soup made with up to a dozen local vegetables sliced in thin strips.

Soupe au fruit à pain—breadfruit soup with onion and celery.

And everywhere, excellent soups made of whichever fish the boats brought in that day.

Main Courses

Matoutou de crabes (sometimes *matété*)—sautéed crab meat with onions, garlic, hot pepper, lemon juice, thyme and other seasonings.

Crabes aux ti bananes vertes —boiled crab and green bananas with an aromatic sauce.

Ouassous—giant riverine crayfish *(écrevisses),* a great delicacy that is becoming rare in the FWI.

Lambi—conch, the Caribbean's favorite mollusk, extracted from its large, attractive shell, tenderized, cut up and served boiled or sautéed in oil with lemon, garlic and assorted seasonings. (FWI fishermen today still blow through the conch shell to let their families and customers know they're heading home—just as the Carib Indians did.)

Blaff—stewed or "soused" fish (very fresh) with lemon or

Lobster Look-Alike

Anglo-Saxon tourists may rejoice when they see "lobster" in English on many FWI menus—often for a reasonable price by Caribbean standards. It is, of course, crawfish or spiny lobster, not the true lobster which it otherwise resembles. Apparently North Americans are presumed not to know the difference, but not so the French—it's always forthrightly *langouste* (crawfish) never *homard* (lobster) on their side of the menu.

You'll find it served cold in salads, perhaps with avocado, or grilled and served with butter, lemon or mayonnaise. This Caribbean crustacean may lack the lobster's delectable claws, but from the kitchen of a French-Creole chef you'll find it almost as exciting.

Fresh? It's just 50 yards from the ocean to this crawfish grill.

lime, garlic, hot red pepper, India wood *(bois d'Inde)* and other spices.

Court-bouillon à la Créole— fish slices marinated in lemon, crushed garlic, hot pepper and salt, then boiled with chives, tomatoes, more garlic and lemon and *fines herbes*.

Calalou—the French-island version of this fragrant, soupy stew prepared throughout the West Indies contains smoked ham, bacon or crab with chives, onions, parsley and special *calalou* greens, garlic and hot pepper. In Père Labat's time, islanders used up to 22 ingredients. This dish, spelled *kallaloo* in the Virgin Islands, is called "pepperpot" elsewhere in the Antilles.

Ti nin lan morue *(bananes vertes et de la morue)*—a typical Creole creation of both Martinique and Guadeloupe including green bananas, cod, sweet potatoes, piquant green peppers, cucumbers and garlic-laced bits of pork, among other things served in separate bowls. Filling and very thirst-provoking.

Anguille (eel) come in many varieties and are enthusiastically snapped up by chefs and housewives when fishing boats bring them in. They're prepared in the usual delectable French manner.

Oursins (sea urchins) are also very common; only the white *oursin* is eaten—in *blaff*, tarts, fritters and omelets.

Note: In Martinique, all fish (except for *blaff*) are first marinated in lime juice, chives, onion, garlic, hot peppers, cloves, *bois d'Inde* and other local spices—and only then cooked. Similar marinades are the rule elsewhere in the French West Indies, which is why the fish tastes so delicious. Also, it's believed in the Caribbean that warm water fish are more flavorsome than their northern cousins. Depending on the season, you'll be eating such freshly caught delights as red snapper *(vivaneau)*, yellowtail *(colas)*, tuna, kingfish *(tazar)*, bonito and smaller fry including silvery *coulirou*.

Dessert

Look for the Creole specialty, a hot tart of grated coconut and delicate pastry. Coconut cake is another favorite, and there are creamy French-style *pâtisserie* products. You may be lucky enough to be offered sherbet of fresh coconut or pineapple, perhaps topped with whipped cream or cold chocolate sauce. Among the array of fruits, cantaloupes are in season early in the year and can be excellent.

Since French cheese travels well, even into the tropics, you'll find a surprising variety from the provinces of the mainland.

Snacks
Mostly in deference to tourists from North America, the FWI have a few snack bars that produce approximations of the

They still talk about the Englishman who always dressed for lunch.

U.S. hamburger. They also serve "hotdogs" and they mean it—the obligatory mustard inside the long white bun in blazing hot!

Drinks

Unless it's their beautiful women and children, the greatest pride of the French West Indians must be their rum; or, their rums—the alcoholic spin-off from their fields of sugarcane.

Ti punch, Creole for *petit punch*, is just that. No relation to punch as it springs to North American minds, this omnipresent drink is a short snort of rum, sugarcane syrup and a dash of lime. On Guadeloupe the accepted proportion is two-thirds rum, one-third syrup. On Martinique, four-fifths rum, one-fifth syrup. Often they'll place a bottle of rum and another of syrup on your table and let you measure it out yourself. There are rituals: Guadeloupean punch drinkers say you shouldn't add lime, lemon or any fruit when dark, old *(vieux)* rum is used, only with white, young, *(jeune)* rum. Purists insist an ice cube will destroy the punch's delicately balanced bouquet. Though most common as an aperitif, punch is the Creole early-morning pick-me-up, the late-night cordial and the most frequent drink with a meal.

More predictable for foreigners are the other rum punches that are long drinks: *planteurs* (with fruit juices), *au coco* (with coconut milk), *aux goyaves* (guava), etc., and the daiquiri.

Sadly, the FWI's *rhum agricole*, more or less straight from the first cane juice, does not make a very satisfactory *piña colada*, that frothy, frosty Puerto Rican blend of industrial rum, cream of coconut, pineapple juice and crushed ice that is the Caribbean's star refreshment.

Tourists will find Martinique and Guadeloupe bars stocked with better known whiskeys, vodkas and gins and on the islands generally, there is a greater choice of French wines than anywhere else in the hemisphere.

During sugarcane-cutting season, street vendors sell straight cane juice for a few francs per glass. It is thick, predictably sweet and non-alcoholic. All year you'll find good bottled fruit drinks and familiar colas. Some French mineral waters are available, a treat for their legions of fans. But local *eaux minérales* are also very good, particularly Martinique's Didier.

To Help You Order...

Could we have a table?   **Pouvons-nous avoir une table?**
Do you have a set menu?   **Avez-vous un menu du jour?**

I'd like a/an/some…   **Je désire…**

beer	**une bière**	mineral water	**de l'eau minérale**
butter	**du beurre**		
bread	**du pain**	potatoes	**des pommes de terre**
coffee	**un café**		
dessert	**un dessert**	salad	**une salade**
fish	**du poisson**	soup	**de la soupe**
fruit	**un fruit**	sugar	**du sucre**
ice-cream	**une glace**	tea	**du thé**
meat	**de la viande**	(iced) water	**de l'eau (glacée)**
menu	**la carte**		
milk	**du lait**	wine	**du vin**

…and Read the Menu

agneau	lamp	**foie**	liver
ail	garlic	**fraises**	strawberries
ananas	pineapple	**framboises**	raspberries
artichauds	artichoke	**gigot**	leg
asperges	asparagus	**haricots verts**	string beans
aubergines	eggplant	**jambon**	ham
bifteck	steak	**langue**	tongue
bœuf	beef	**lapin**	rabbit
canard	duck	**melon**	melon (cantaloupe)
carottes	carrots		
chou	cabbage	**moutarde**	mustard
chou-fleur	cauliflower	**nouilles**	noodles
choux de Bruxelles	brussels sprouts	**oignons**	onions
		petits pois	peas
concombre	cucumber	**pommes**	apples
côtelettes	chops, cutlet	**porc**	pork
courgettes	baby marrow (zucchini)	**poulet**	chicken
		raisins	grapes
endive	chicory (endive)	**saucisse/ saucisson**	sausage
épinards	spinach	**saumon**	salmon
flageolets	beans	**veau**	veal

FWI: Facts and Figures

Geography: The islands of the FWI belong to the Lesser Antilles chain. Situated about 100 miles apart, the main islands are Guadeloupe (530 square miles), which consists of two islets separated by a salt-water channel called the Rivière Salée, and Martinique (425 square miles). The smaller islands of La Désirade, Marie-Galante and Les Saintes lie just east and south of Guadeloupe; Saint-Martin and Saint-Barthélemy are some 160 miles to the north. Each island has a gentle Caribbean, and a more rugged Atlantic coast. Guadeloupe's volcano, La Soufrière, rises to a height of 4,813 feet, while Martinique's Mount Pelée reaches to 4,700 feet.

Population: Over 650,000, including Blacks, Creoles, Mulattoes and Asian Indians.

Principal cities: Pointe-à-Pitre (population 100,000) is Guadeloupe's largest city, while little Basse-Terre serves as the capital. With a population of around 100,000, Fort-de-France is capital and commercial center of Martinique. Among other main towns are the small ports of Marigot (Saint-Martin) and Gustavia (Saint-Barthélemy).

Government: The French West Indies comprise two overseas *régions* of France: that of Guadeloupe (including its island dependencies of Saint-Martin, Saint-Barthélemy, La Désirade, Les Saintes and Marie-Galante) and Martinique. *Préfets* appointed by the French Minister of the Interior administer the affairs of each region, which sends three deputies and two senators to the parliament in Paris. The locally elected legislative bodies are known as the General and Regional Councils. The Economic and Social Committee plays a consultative role.

Industries: Agriculture (sugar, bananas, pineapple, rum, coffee, cocoa, spices) and tourism.

Religion: Predominantly Roman Catholic.

Language: French, Creole. English widely understood in tourist centers.

BLUEPRINT for a Perfect Trip

How to Get There

Owing to the complexity and variability of the many fares available, you should seek the advice of an informed travel agent well before your departure.

BY AIR

Scheduled Flights

From North America. Direct service operates several times a week to Martinique from various U.S. cities, mainly in the northeast and midwest, and from Montreal and Toronto in Canada. There are also convenient flights to Guadeloupe from a selection of cities in the U.S. and Canada, while direct service to Saint-Martin and Saint-Barthelemy is more limited.

Miami, New York and San Juan (Puerto Rico) provide logical connecting points for travelers not on a direct line to the French West Indies.

From Great Britain and Eire. There are no direct flights from Great Britain or Eire to the French West Indies. You can, however, fly via Paris to Guadeloupe and Martinique. Another possibility is to travel directly from Heathrow to Antigua (U.K.), continuing to the French West Indies on inter-Caribbean services (see section below). Of course, it is also possible to travel to a gateway city in North America and pick up a flight to the French West Indies there.

Inter-island Flights. Daily flights link Martinique and Guadeloupe, and there is service daily or many times a week from both islands to Puerto Rico, Antigua, Saint-Martin and Saint-Barthelemy (which can also be reached via St. Thomas, U.S. Virgin Islands).

Charter Flights and Package Tours

From North America. Many attractive tour packages and charters are on offer. Look into the One-Stop Inclusive Tour Charter (OTC) packages which combine air travel with hotel and other ground arrangements at bargain prices.

From Great Britain and Eire. While no charter flights operate to the French West Indies from British or Irish airports, there are a number of travel agents who can organize any kind of tour for you and may have package deals available.

BY SEA

From North America. A number of Caribbean cruises leave from Miami, New York and San Juan and stop at one or more ports in the French West Indies.

From Great Britain and Eire. Although there are no cruises departing from the British Isles, you can sail from Le Havre to Fort-de-France or Pointe-à-Pitre on banana boats (10 passengers maximum) on which you will be offered the same accommodation as on line boats.

You can also take a fly-cruise package; you fly to Fort-de-France or Pointe-à-Pitre and cruise around the Caribbean islands, stopping at one or more ports in the French West Indies. You may also fly to New York, Miami or San Juan and connect with a cruise there.

Note: Most airlines and travel agents refuse to sell one-way tickets to any Caribbean island, in accordance with declared (if only sporadically enforced) requirements by many governments that travelers arrive with a round trip or continuing ticket.

When to Go

The French West Indies enjoy a tropical climate all year, the trade winds ensuring that it's never too hot. So close to the equator, there's remarkably little temperature variation, with no proper seasons. But from May to November, it tends to be rather warmer, certainly wetter and sometimes stormy. Nonetheless, rain tends to pass quickly and you should have sunshine practically every day.

Carême (Lent)—from January to April—is the driest and relatively coolest period. It's also the height of the tourist season, meaning significantly more expensive hotel prices, not to mention restaurants and shops crowded with vacationers.

In the breezy mountains it's usually several degrees cooler than by the seashore. The two small northern FWI—Saint-Martin and Saint-Barthélemy—are slightly windier and a shade cooler than Guadeloupe and Martinique.

The official hurricane season is from June 1 to November 30, but only an average of six hurricanes blow through the Caribbean each year—and thanks to satellite forecasts and weather flights, they no longer come as a surprise.

The following temperature charts will give you a more precise idea of conditions to expect:

		J	F	M	A	M	J	J	A	S	O	N	D
Air temperature	F	76	76	76	78	79	80	81	81	80	79	78	77
	C	24	24	24	25	26	27	27	27	27	26	26	25
Sea temperature	F	72	73	75	77	77	77	79	79	77	77	77	75
	C	22	23	24	25	25	25	26	26	25	25	25	24

Figures shown are approximate monthly averages.

An A-Z Summary of Practical Information and Facts

> Listed after many entries is the appropriate French translation, usually in the singular, plus a number of phrases that should help you when seeking assistance.

ACCOMMODATIONS. See also CAMPING. The French West Indies offers a wide range of resort accommodation, as well as a large number of rooms for visitors in private villas and bungalows. This represents a huge increase since 1970 when tourism began to grow here.

French government hotel ratings run from four-star de luxe down through three-star, two-star, etc. The great majority of hotels are small, many of them family-run. Not all establishments are rated, which does not necessarily mean you should avoid them. Tourist offices in Pointe-à-Pitre and Fort-de-France have up-to-date lists of hotels, prices and addresses of vacant apartments or bungalows for rent.

Tourist hotels are usually on the coast, though some of the most pleasant perch on hilltops or mountainsides looking down over the sea. As they're rather isolated you'll probably take many meals where you're staying. Larger towns have a few small commercial hotels for those who like metropolitan bustle.

Prices are 40% higher during the high season (mid-December to mid-April), and reservations are a must. During the other eight months there's plenty of hotel space available at lower prices. Single rooms may be 80% of the double room rate. The 10% service charge is not always included in quoted prices. Your hotel could insist upon any of the following plans:

EP   – European Plan (room only)
CP   – Continental Plan (room and breakfast, continental or American)
MAP – Modified American Plan (room, breakfast and dinner)
AP   – American Plan (room and three meals)

a double/single room/room with a double bed	une chambre à deux lits/à un lit/ avec un grand lit
with/without bath	avec/sans bain
What's the rate per night?	Combien demandez-vous pour une nuit?

A AIRPORTS *(aéroport)*

One of the Caribbean's best, the modern Raizet airport on **Guadeloupe** is equipped to handle the largest jets. It's about 2 miles from Pointe-à-Pitre, 5 miles from the Gosier resort area, but significantly farther from other hotels. There is a public bus service between the Le Raizet district and Pointe-à-Pitre. The buses run about every 15 minutes. Taxis (expensive!) are also available. For further information, ask at the airport's welcome desk.

The airport has baggage carts (free) and a few porters. There is also a post-telegraph office, a bank for currency exchange (open Monday through Saturday) and a large air-conditioned transit bar and lounge with duty-free counters offering a wide choice of items.

At Les Saintes, Baillif, Marie-Galante and Désirade there are small-plane airstrips.

Martinique's Lamentin airport has fewer facilities than Raizet but also handles jumbo jets. It's about 5 miles from Fort-de-France. Taxi rates, posted at the baggage claim area, are high. There's no airport bus, but (though it's not advertised) you could cross the highway and get a *taxi collectif* to town—though it's not always easy. There are motorcoaches available for groups only.

Lamentin has baggage carts and porters, a useful tourist information counter (English is spoken), and an open-air departure lounge where French cheeses, *pâtés,* wines and other duty-free items are sold.

At both Raizet and Lamentin there are restaurants, baggage lockers and car-rental desks. The banks at both airports may give a slightly better rate in French francs for other currencies than banks in town do.

Saint-Martin's French side has only the tiny Espérance airport served by small planes from Guadeloupe and Saint-Barthélemy. Juliana airport on the Dutch side takes international jets. It is about 6 miles from Marigot to Juliana, and easy to fix a taxi ride during the daytime between the two airports. Juliana has duty-free counters (prices identical with the rest of the island), shops, bar and snack bar as well as car-rental representatives. But note that your rented car will be delivered to your hotel; you may not pick it up at the airport.

Saint-Barthélemy's modern international airport has a bar, restaurant, shops and car rental agencies.

French West Indies airports charge no departure tax, but Juliana on the Dutch side of Saint-Martin charges a small fee.

Where's the bus for...?   **D'où part le bus pour...?**

BABY-SITTERS. Your hotel can probably arrange for one, often a maid or a student. In some towns the day-nursery service *(crèche)* will provide sitters.

Can you get me/us a baby-sitter for tonight?	**Pouvez-vous me/nous trouver une baby-sitter pour ce soir?**

CAMPING *(camping).* Guadeloupe has one organized campsite, and backpacking is permitted on public beaches and in the Natural Park. Martinique allows camping almost everywhere and has a number of sites with facilities. In Fort-de-France you can buy or rent camping equipment. Saint-Martin permits camping but there are no organized sites. Saint-Barthélemy does not allow any camping. You can get further details from any town hall.

Do you have room for a tent?	**Avez-vous de la place pour une tente?**
May we camp here, please?	**Pouvons-nous camper ici, s'il vous plaît?**

CAR RENTAL and DRIVING

Rental *(location de voitures).* The auto-rental business flourishes throughout the French West Indies with rates which will surprise many visitors. Most cars for rent are French, but there are also German, Italian and Japanese models. Few have automatic transmission or air-conditioning. Companies often levy a mileage (per-kilometer) charge as well as a basic daily fee for short-term rentals, with insurance added. A deposit is normally required. You must have a valid driver's license and be at least 21. Many firms accept major credit cards.

On the road. It may be officially denied, but an occasional cow or goat does wander onto Martinique's grand superhighway *(autoroute)* which starts outside Fort-de-France. Roads in the FWI range from very good to very rutted. They wind and climb over the countless hills, often with blind curves. To speed is to court disaster, as you'll be sharing the road with other tourists as well as farm carts, animals and huge tractor-carriers full of sugarcane.

The worst hazards are the deep drainage ditches lining many roads. Although they are necessary because of the torrential rains which occasionally fall, these ditches often appear unexpectedly along narrow roads, with nothing but your skill to keep your car out of them.

C

There are a few familiar international road signs, but generally curves and other particularities go unannounced. So do indications to towns and villages of the FWI. But people will be delighted to point places out to you, or to hop in and take you where you're heading. You say *Bonjour* first, then ask for your destination.

Fluid measures

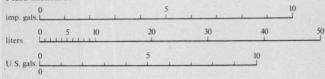

Distance

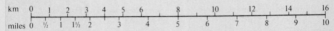

I'd like to rent a car (tomorrow).	**Je voudrais louer une voiture (demain).**
for one day/a week	**pour une journée/une semaine**
Please include full insurance.	**Avec assurance tous risques, s'il vous plaît.**
(international) driving license	**permis de conduire (international)**
car registration papers	**permis de circulation**
Are we on the right road for...?	**Sommes-nous sur la route de...?**
Full tank, please.	**Le plein, s'il vous plaît.**
regular/super	**normale/super**
Check the oil/tires/battery.	**Veuillez contrôler l'huile/les pneus/la batterie.**
I've had a breakdown.	**Ma voiture est en panne.**
There's been an accident.	**Il y a eu un accident.**

CIGARETTES, CIGARS, TOBACCO (*cigarettes, cigares, tabac*). Duty-free American or English cigarettes on Saint-Martin and St. Barts are quite a bargain; on Martinique and Guadeloupe, however, prices are double, and for best value for money, stay with French brands. Cuban cigars are available—for those that can afford them—but blends from other countries cost less. Pipe tobacco is more expensive on Martinique and Guadeloupe than in the U.S.

A pack of cigarettes/A box of matches, please.	**Un paquet de cigarettes/Une boîte d'allumettes, s'il vous plaît.**
light tobacco	**du tabac blond**
dark tobacco	**du tabac brun**
filter-tipped	**avec filtre**
without filter	**sans filtre**

CLOTHING. Local people consider appearance important: slovenly, or flashy but tasteless dressing is looked down upon, even though casual clothes are definitely the thing. Casual but smart, would seem to best define what you'll need: Paris sets the tone, after all... The casinos don't insist on either jacket or necktie, except on Dutch Saint-Martin. Women may want to take long skirts for evenings, and sandals as well as comfortable walking shoes are essential for everyone.

Nude bathing is quite commonplace on Guadeloupe, less so on Martinique, but in any case should be kept to hotel areas, as islanders still are not quite used to the habit.

COMMUNICATIONS

Mail, telegrams, telex. Since urban post offices in the FWI are out of reach of most resort areas, you'll rely on your hotel desk for routine postal matters. That may include telegrams, telexes and international phone calls directed through the French government postal system.

However, Fort-de-France and Pointe-à-Pitre have large central post offices (with public telex), and there are branch offices in smaller towns where you can send mail or telegrams.

The French postal service usually functions marvelously in the FWI. Airmail from either Europe or the United States should reach your hotel within 4 or 5 days.

It's better to have people back home spell out "French West Indies" after the name of your island—letters are occasionally returned to sender by baffled American post offices not used to the abbreviation "FWI".

Telephone. Much of the FWI now has direct-dial local telephone, including an automatic link between Martinique and Guadeloupe. There is good English-speaking operator service from the islands to either Europe or North America. At peak periods you might have to **111**

wait as long as half an hour. Phone connections between the French and Dutch sides of Saint-Martin, where it's authoritatively rumored there's only one line, have traditionally been almost hopeless.

special delivery (express)	**exprès**
airmail	**par avion**
registered	**recommandé**
A stamp for this letter/ postcard, please.	**Un timbre pour cette lettre/ carte postale, s'il vous plaît.**
I want to send a telegram to...	**J'aimerais envoyer un télégramme à...**
Have you any mail for...?	**Avez-vous du courrier pour...?**
Can you get me this number in...?	**Pouvez-vous me donner ce numéro à...?**

COMPLAINTS *(réclamation)*. The owner or manager of the hotel, restaurant or other enterprise is your first resort should you feel you've been wronged. Otherwise, the Guadeloupe and Martinique Office du Tourisme (see TOURIST INFORMATION OFFICES) exist to help visitors sort out any problems. They both have English-speaking personnel.

CONSULATES *(consulat)*

Great Britain/Canada: Pointe Jarry, Baie-Mahault, Guadeloupe; tel. 26 64 29.

U.S.A.: 10 Rue Schoelcher, Martinique; tel. 63 13 03.

Where's the... consulate?	**Où se trouve le consulat...?**
American/British/Canadian	**américain/britannique/canadien**

CONVERTER CHARTS. For fluid and distance measures, see page 110. France uses the metric system.

Temperature

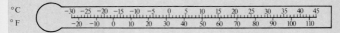

Length

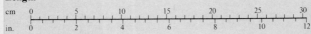

C

meters 0   1 m   2 m

ft./yd. 0   1 ft.   1 yd.   2 yd.

Weight

grams 0   100   200   300   400   500   600   700   800   900   1 kg

oz.   0   4   8   12   1 lb.   20   24   28   2 lb.

CRIME and THEFT. Here's some of the very best news about the French West Indies: any sort of violation of the law is extremely rare. No dangerous hoodlums here, no violent assaults. A crime wave is as unthinkable as a snowstorm. If there's any petty theft, it would probably be of a lobster trap rather than a tourist's handbag. This is not to suggest you abandon common sense about your property, of course. Leave all valuables in your hotel safe-deposit box.

I want to report a theft.   **J'aimerais déclarer un vol.**

CUSTOMS *(douane)* **and ENTRY REGULATIONS.** The following chart shows what main duty-free items you may take into the FWI and, when returning home, into your own country:

Into:	Cigarettes		Cigars		Tobacco	Spirits		Wine
FWI [1])	400		100		500 g.	1 l.		2 l.
[2])	300	or	75	or	400 g.	1½ l.	and	5 l.
[3])	200		50		250 g.	1 l.		2 l.
Canada	200	and	50	and	900 g.	1.1 l.	or	1.1 l.
Eire	200	or	50	or	250 g.	1 l.	and	2 l.
U.K.	200	or	50	or	250 g.	1 l.	and	2 l.
U.S.A.	200	and	100	and	[4])	1 l.	or	1 l.

[1]) Visitors arriving from outside Europe
[2]) Visitors arriving from EEC countries with non duty-free items
[3]) Visitors arriving from EEC countries with duty-free items and visitors from other European countries
[4]) A reasonable quantity

113

C North American citizens need only a passport that has expired by a maximum of 5 years, together with a birth certificate or voters card for a stay in the FWI of up to three weeks; a visa will be issued on arrival. Longer than that you'll need a valid passport. British nationals may enter with a national identity card, without a visa. Smallpox vaccination certificates are not required for North American visitors nor those from Great Britain. All visitors must be in possession of a return or onward ticket.

Currency restrictions. There's no limit on the importation or exportation of local or foreign currencies or traveller's cheques, but amounts in excess of 50,000 francs or its equivalent must be declared.

I've nothing to declare.	**Je n'ai rien à déclarer.**
It's for my own use.	**C'est pour mon usage personnel.**

D **DRUGS.** Use of illegal narcotics is practically non-existent in the FWI. Police are vigilant, penalties severe.

E **ELECTRIC CURRENT.** As in France 220-volt, 50-cycle current is used, though you may also encounter 110 volts. Many hotels provide converters.

an adaptor plug/a battery	**une prise complémentaire/une pile**

EMERGENCIES (*urgence*). The following numbers will be useful in case of accident, injury or sudden illness:

	Guadeloupe	Martinique
Police	82 00 05 (Pointe-à-Pitre) 81 11 55 (Basse-Terre)	17 (Fort-de-France)
Gendarmerie	82 09 20 (Pointe-à-Pitre) 81 10 35 (Basse-Terre)	71 51 35 (Fort-de-France)
Ambulance	82 46 46 (Pointe-à-Pitre)	71 59 48 (Fort-de-France)
Fire	82 00 28 (Pointe-à-Pitre) 81 11 91 (Basse-Terre)	18 (Fort-de-France)

GUIDES and INTERPRETERS *(guide; interprète)*. Tour agencies provide English-speaking guides for group excursions, but there are no organized agencies with interpreters, guides or translators for individual tourists. Exceptionally it may be possible to hire someone from a travel agency or the Centre d'Etude des Langues, part of the Chamber of Commerce, but this is not a regular service, and it is likely to be expensive.

HAIRDRESSERS *(coiffeur)*. FWI barber shops are often modest establishments by British and North American standards. Women's hairdressers tend to be rather popular social meeting places, so it's wise to book ahead.

A 10 to 15% tip is usual.

I'd like...	**Je voudrais...**
a haircut	**une coupe de cheveux**
a shampoo and set	**un shampooing et mise en plis**
a blow-dry	**un brushing**
the color chart	**le nuancier**
a color rinse/a hair-dye	**un rinçage/une teinture**
Don't cut it too short (here).	**Pas trop court (ici), s'il vous plaît.**
A little more off (here).	**Un peu plus court (ici).**

HEALTH and SAFETY. See also MEDICAL CARE and EMERGENCIES. These islands are marvelous for your health, but the tropical sun deserves your fullest respect. To bask for more than half an hour on your first day in the FWI could ruin your vacation. Even after you've achieved a basic tan, you can suffer sunstroke from over-exposure (this goes for anyone of any age). That's why you shouldn't stay out for hours during the hottest period of the day; that's also why a straw hat is such a good investment!

For those who go back and forth between icy air-conditioning and the beach, the common cold is frequent. To avoid the risk try to avoid air-conditioning—the island's breezes are cooling enough without help from electric appliances, particularly at night.

As throughout the Caribbean, certain fish may cause serious food poisoning called *ciguatera*. Before consuming anything you catch, be sure to check with local experts.

Although no incidents concerning sharks have been reported around the French Caribbean shores, it's important to remember never to swim

H after dark anywhere in the Caribbean, and while snorkeling or scuba diving don't wear shiny objects such as watches or jewelry.

Beware of spiky black sea urchins on the sea bottom which can inflict a painful puncture on unwary swimmers.

With all those dense forests, you'd think danger menaced from every branch and that snakes abound. Not so—Guadeloupe and her subsidiary islands have no poisonous snakes or other dangerous animals. Martinique does, however, have poisonous vipers called *trigonocéphales* or *fer de lance* in banana groves, sugar-cane fields and the tropical forest. None of the many lizards you'll see are harmful—in fact they're very useful for consuming mosquitos and other insects. On the beach, especially late in the afternoon, you may encounter the tiny sand flies known as *gniens-gniens*. Retreat is the only defense.

Signs should warn you not to touch or approach the *mancenillier* (manchineel) tree which has poisonous greenish, apple-like fruit.

Another little-discussed hazard: swimming in rivers or ponds. The dangerous bilharzia parasite can be picked up in certain streams and pools; be wary, as there is no indication of the menace anywhere.

HITCH-HIKING *(auto-stop).* Legal, safe and often speedy, this is a popular way to get around in the FWI. If you rent a car, you'll probably soon find yourself giving rides to hikers.

Can you give me a lift to...?   **Pouvez-vous m'emmener à...?**

I **ISLAND-HOPPING.** There's nothing like it if you're on a yacht or sailboat. If not, there's limited boat service along the Antilles chain, and local airlines run daily scheduled flights to and from the islands. One potential problem is that you probably won't be able to buy a one-way ticket to another island. The authorities are glad to have tourists come and visit, but don't want to see them stay too long as unemployment is high. So they require that you have a round-trip ticket.

You can also hire a yacht on the spot, with or without crew. Local yacht-rental firms (or Paris-based companies) can organize cruises which include full board, excursions to the islands and evening entertainment.

For regular scheduled boat services, see under TRANSPORTATION.

L **LANGUAGE.** Very French, these West Indies are, so that every school-child is taught the language of Balzac and Baudelaire. But not so French that they speak it among themselves. For everyday purposes, within and without the family, *créole* is widely used on Martinique and Guadeloupe. It's rather different on Saint-Martin where the islanders' speech has been influenced by many immigrants. On little St. Barts, where everything is very different, the dialect is a bewildering mixture of old French with Swedish, English, etc.

It's said that the colorful Creole dialect derives from the simplified communication originally used between French planters and the newly arrived African slaves. It's a graphic and very simple dialect with no grammar or syntax. Even the islanders consider it an amusing language—you can't be serious in Creole, they say.

Some common French phrases, followed by Creole, which may help you break the ice or simply be polite:

Good morning, good afternoon	**Bonjour**	*Bonjou*
Good evening	**Bonsoir**	*Bonsouè*
Goodbye	**Au revoir**	*Au vouè*
How are you?	**Comment allez-vous?**	*Ka ou fè*
Please	**S'il vous plaît**	*Souplé*
Thank you	**Merci**	*Messi*
You're welcome	**Je vous en prie**	*Pa ni ayen adan ça*

LAUNDRY and DRY CLEANING *(blanchisserie; nettoyage à sec)*. There are reasonably-priced laundromats, laundries and dry-cleaning establishments in the large towns, but most hotels are out in the country, so it's more convenient to let them take care of your clothes-cleaning problems.

LOST AND FOUND. Whatever you lose, your chances are excellent of having it returned. Taxi drivers have been known to call half a dozen hotels, seeking tourists who've left something in their cabs. Restaurants will unfailingly have your camera or guide-book waiting when you return to ask for it.

If your youngster wanders off the beach or out of the store where you're shopping, friendly islanders will take him in hand, and by checking at the more obvious places you'll surely find the young adventurer.

I've lost my wallet/handbag/passport. **J'ai perdu mon portefeuille/sac/passeport.**

M   **MAPS.** There are excellent maps of the FWI published by the Institut Géographique National. You should order number 510 for Guadeloupe and number 511 for Martinique. Adequate street plans of Fort-de-France and Pointe-à-Pitre are available at tourist information offices.

a street plan of...	**un plan de la ville de...**
a map of this island	**une carte routière de l'île**

MEDICAL CARE. Make certain your health insurance will cover you while you're abroad and then relax and enjoy your vacation. If your home insurance cannot be extended to foreign countries, you may want to take out special travel insurance to pay for accident, illness or hospitalization for the duration of your trip.

The major islands have hospitals and clinics, and your hotel will know how to get a doctor quickly.

Drugstores *(pharmacie)* in the larger towns operate on a rotating basis so that at least one is always open. Those, and the names of doctors on duty off-hours *(service de garde)* are listed in the Martinique or Guadeloupe editions of the daily local newspaper *France-Antilles*. Drugstores stock primarily French and Swiss medicine. See also HEALTH AND SAFETY.

I need a doctor.	**Il me faut un médecin.**
I've a pain here.	**J'ai mal ici.**
a dentist	**un dentiste**
an upset stomach	**mal à l'estomac**
a fever	**de la fièvre**
sunburn	**un coup de soleil**

MEETING PEOPLE. Women in the FWI complain that they outnumber the men because unemployment has driven so many men in search of work elsewhere. But this doesn't mean that visiting men will meet local girls socially. In discotheques for example, FWI girls don't normally dance with strangers, simply because they're serious about their dancing and don't enjoy doing it with a novice.

Tourists, however, have a good chance of meeting each other in the hotel cocktail lounges or nightclubs.

In this relaxed society, conventions are anything but rigid. With one major exception—you the visitor, shopper, arriving guest, must make the first polite move toward an islander, by simply saying either *Bonjour* or *Bonsoir*. Otherwise you'll probably be considered impolite (see also LANGUAGE).

If you're invited to someone's home, flowers are appreciated.

MONEY MATTERS

Currency. The french *franc* (abbreviated *F* or *FF*) is divided into 100 *centimes (cts)*. The coins and banknotes in circulation in the FWI are exactly the same as those used in France.

Coins: 5, 10, 20, 50 cts; 1, 2, 5, 10 F
Banknotes: 20, 50, 100, 200, 500 F

For currency restrictions, see CUSTOMS AND ENTRY REGULATIONS.

Banks and currency-exchange offices *(banque; bureau de change).* Banking hours vary slightly from island to island, but they are usually from 8 a.m. to 3 p.m. in summer and from 8 a.m. to noon and 2.30 to 4 p.m. in winter, Monday through Friday. They close on the afternoon preceding a public holiday (see PUBLIC HOLIDAYS). All banks change traveler's checks and currency.

Credit cards and traveler's checks *(carte de crédit; chèque de voyage* or *traveller's chèque).* Many FWI hotels, shops, car-rental firms, and some restaurants accept major credit cards, while you will be able to use your traveler's checks practically everywhere. Note that for all non-residents a 20% discount for purchases made with traveler's checks is common in Pointe-à-Pitre shops; the same discount is extended to cover credit-card acquisitions in many Martinique stores. Therefore, for shopping on those two islands you won't want to obtain a great many French francs (although you can always reconvert them into other currency such as dollars without significant loss). On Saint-Martin and St. Barts there are no traveler's check or credit card "deals"—you can't get lower than duty-free.

Vacationing Americans should not plan on cashing personal checks on their U.S. banks—it can easily take 10 days or more for a check to clear.

Prices. Except for duty-free shopping on Saint-Martin and Saint-Barthélemy, prices in the FWI are uncomfortably high. Visitors on all-inclusive package tours will notice the inflation least.

Wine and food are often overpriced at restaurants frequented by tourists, and in a top quality restaurant you can find yourself paying horrendous prices for a four-course meal. Eating *à la carte* too often can ruin an average vacation budget, especially in French restaurants where the justification for the high prices is that everything has to be imported. The many Creole restaurants charge somewhat less, as do the other non-French establishments in the islands.

I want to change some dollars/ pounds.	**Je voudrais changer des dollars/ livres sterling.**

M **MOTORSCOOTER RENTAL** *(location de motocyclettes)*. On the major islands, distances are too great (and the sun too hot) for scooters to be very useful or comfortable. However, in a few places you should be able to rent a motorscooter.

N **NEWSPAPERS and MAGAZINES** *(journal; revue)*. The only English-language newspaper normally available in the FWI is the *International Herald Tribune,* flown in one day late from Paris. Major American news magazines are on sale in Pointe-à-Pitre and Fort-de-France. French publications are, of course, available, as well as *France-Antilles,* the only local daily paper.

Have you any English-language newspapers?	**Avez-vous des journaux en anglais?**

P **PETS.** You can take your dog or cat with you on vacation in the FWI if you present either a health certificate issued within 5 days before departure, stating that the country of origin has been free of rabies for 3 years or proof the pet had an antirabies shot not less than a month nor more than a year previously. Check to be sure your hotel will accept your pet.

PHOTOGRAPHY. Except on the duty-free islands, film prices are very high in the FWI. It's cheaper to buy film at home. Slides are usually sent to France for processing, meaning a considerable delay. Other film is developed and printed locally.

To ensure good color transparencies in the blazing sunlight you must use a skylight or similar filters. You'll probably get best seashore and outdoor results late in the afternoon.

North American tourists who own relatively new, expensive cameras might want to register their serial numbers with U.S. customs before traveling to the Caribbean in order to avoid any costly misunderstandings upon return home.

Some airport security machines use X-rays which can ruin your film. Ask that it be checked separately, or enclose it in a lead-lined bag.

a black-and-white film	**un film noir et blanc**
a film for color prints	**un film couleurs**
a color-slide film	**un film de diapositives**
a 35-mm film	**un film de trente-cinq millimètres**
May I take a picture?	**Puis-je prendre une photo?**

POLICE. French *gendarmes* and security police, usually wearing khaki shorts, operate courteously and efficiently in the FWI. See also EMERGENCIES.

PUBLIC HOLIDAYS *(jour férié)*. These are the main national holidays. See page 91 for details of other local celebrations and events.

January 1	Jour de l'An	New Year's Day
May 1	Fête du Travail	Labor Day
May 8	Armistice 1945	Victory Day
July 14	Fête Nationale	Bastille Day
July 21	Schoelcher	Schoelcher Day
August 15	Assomption	Assumption Day
November 1	Toussaint	All Saints' Day
November 2	Jour des Morts	All Soul's Day
November 11	Anniversaire de l'Armistice	Armistice Day
December 25	Noël	Christmas Day
Movable dates:	Lundi de Pâques	Easter Monday
	Ascension	Ascension
	Lundi de Pentecôte	Whit Monday

RADIO and TV. Dozens of radio stations broadcast in English on medium wave. Americans with short-wave radios can hear a selection of major network newscasts and commentaries on the Armed Forces Radio & Television Service (AFRTS) in the morning and evening. The BBC World Service can be heard clearly day and night, either on short wave or relayed by British Caribbean islands radio.

The FWI have two TV channels.

RELIGIOUS SERVICES *(office religieux)*. Between 80 and 90% of the French West Indians are Roman Catholic, and you'll find mass is celebrated wherever you are on the islands. Saturday evening is almost as popular a time for mass as Sunday morning. There are also many Protestant denominations which hold regular services that your hotel can inform you about. Times are also listed in weekly tourist information booklets published on the major islands. The radio stations have religious programs every day of the year.

S **SIESTA.** In the wise fashion of the tropics, the French islands shut down almost completely in the early afternoon for two or three hours. A long lunch by the sea and a nap under a coconut tree should get you through these hottest hours when there's absolutely nothing going on which you might be missing.

T **TIME DIFFERENCES.** The French West Indies remain on Atlantic Standard Time all year. This is one hour ahead of Eastern Standard Time and four hours behind GMT. The FWI and the U.S. east coast are on the same time when Daylight Saving Time is in effect.

Winter time chart				
Los Angeles	Chicago	New York	**FWI**	London
8 a.m.	10 a.m.	11 a.m.	**noon**	4 p.m.

TIPPING. Until recently tipping was considered a sign of disrespect in the FWI. Tourism has been changing that. A 10% tip is now the general norm. However, it's not strictly necessary to tip a taxi driver as the fares are so high. Even your hotel maid may not yet confidently expect a tip, but if you've had good service it's now considered a nice thing to do, and she won't think you're rude as she would have before tourism's "blessings" came to these islands.

Some suggestions:

Hairdresser/Barber	10–15%
Maid, per week	50–100 F (optional)
Porter	5 F
Taxi driver	5% (optional)
Tourist guide	10% (optional)
Waiter	5–10%

TOILETS. You'll find the French word *toilettes* on the door, or man and woman symbols. Public toilets are conveniently located in most towns.

122 Where are the toilets, please? **Où sont les toilettes, s'il vous plaît?**

TOURIST INFORMATION OFFICES

Canada

Montreal: 1981 McGill College Avenue, Esso Tower, Suite 490, Que. H3A 2W9; tel. (514) 288-4264
Toronto: 1 Dundas Street W, Suite 2405, P.O. Box 8, Ont. M5G 1Z3; tel. (416) 593-4717

Great Britain

London: 178, Piccadilly, W1V 0AL; tel. (01) 493-6594

U.S.A.

New York: 610 Fifth Avenue, NY 10020; tel. (212) 757-1125
Chicago: 645 N. Michigan Avenue, Suite 430, IL 60611; tel. (312) 336-6301
Los Angeles: 9401 Wilshire Boulevard, Room 840, Beverly Hills, CA 90212; tel. (213) 272-2661
San Francisco: 1 Hallidie Plaza, CA 94102; tel. (415) 986-4174

Guadeloupe

5, Square de la Banque, B.P. 1099, 97181 Pointe-à-Pitre; tel. 82 09 30

Martinique

Boulevard Alfassa, B.P. 520, 97206 Fort-de-France; tel. 63 79 60

TRANSPORTATION

Buses/Minibuses. Guadeloupe and Saint-Martin have cheap, efficient bus services, and there's a network of minibuses on Saint-Martin.
Martinique's public transportation is primarily by collective taxi. Ten times less expensive than by regular taxi, it's an interesting way to meet the French West Indians who use these minibuses, or jitneys, regularly.

Taxis. Your taxi driver from Guadeloupe's Raizet airport to the hotel may claim his island's cab fares are the highest in the world. The same is true of Martinique. Regular taxis on both islands have fixed rates by distance, posted at such key points as airports and listed in the weekly information brochures. The rates are higher at night. On Saint-Martin and St. Barts, however, taxi fares won't devastate your vacation budget as on the larger islands.

Boat service. From Guadeloupe there is regular motor launch service to Les Saintes early every morning from Trois-Rivières, and on weekday afternoons from Basse-Terre. There are boats from Pointe-à-Pitre to **123**

T Marie-Galante on certain days. On Martinique ferries link Fort-de-France with the Pointe du Bout hotel complex and smaller beach spots further on throughout the day until about midnight. Saint-Martin has boat service to Saint-Barthélemy, Saba and Saint-Eustatius as well as between its own French and Dutch sides. There is also a long-distance cargo and passenger boat which runs from Pointe-à-Pitre to Saint-Martin via Saint-Barthélemy. For information on these services call the Office du Tourisme (82 09 30). See also ISLAND HOPPING.

W WATER *(eau)*. The water's good on all the French islands. If you prefer to drink mineral water instead of tap water, there are good local varieties—carbonated or non-carbonated—as well as popular French brands imported from the Continent. Note that in places where the drinking water is from cisterns (as on St. Barts), it will lack the normal mineral content of well water.

SOME USEFUL EXPRESSIONS

yes/no	**oui/non**
please/thank you	**s'il vous plaît/merci**
excuse me	**excusez-moi**
you're welcome	**je vous en prie**
where/when/how	**où/quand/comment**
how long/how far	**combien de temps/à quelle distance**
yesterday/today/tomorrow	**hier/aujourd'hui/demain**
day/week/month/year	**jour/semaine/mois/année**
left/right	**gauche/droite**
up/down	**en haut/en bas**
big/small	**grand/petit**
cheap/expensive	**bon marché/cher**
open/closed	**ouvert/fermé**
I don't understand.	**Je ne comprends pas.**
What does this mean?	**Que signifie ceci?**
Waiter/Waitress, please!	**S'il vous plaît!**
I'd like...	**J'aimerais...**
How much is that?	**C'est combien?**

124

DAYS OF THE WEEK

Sunday	**dimanche**	Thursday	**jeudi**
Monday	**lundi**	Friday	**vendredi**
Tuesday	**mardi**	Saturday	**samedi**
Wednesday	**mercredi**		

MONTHS

January	**janvier**	July	**juillet**
February	**février**	August	**août**
March	**mars**	September	**septembre**
April	**avril**	October	**octobre**
May	**mai**	November	**novembre**
June	**juin**	December	**décembre**

NUMBERS

0	**zéro**	19	**dix-neuf**
1	**un, une**	20	**vingt**
2	**deux**	21	**vingt et un**
3	**trois**	22	**vingt-deux**
4	**quatre**	23	**vingt-trois**
5	**cinq**	30	**trente**
6	**six**	40	**quarante**
7	**sept**	50	**cinquante**
8	**huit**	60	**soixante**
9	**neuf**	70	**soixante-dix**
10	**dix**	71	**soixante et onze**
11	**onze**	80	**quatre-vingts**
12	**douze**	90	**quatre-vingt-dix**
13	**treize**	100	**cent**
14	**quatorze**	101	**cent un**
15	**quinze**	126	**cent vingt-six**
16	**seize**	200	**deux cents**
17	**dix-sept**	300	**trois cents**
18	**dix-huit**	1000	**mille**

Index

An asterisk (*) next to a page number indicates a map reference. To help readers find a locality on Guadeloupe, the abbreviations GT and BT (Grande-Terre/Basse-Terre) have been used.

Abymes, Les (Guadeloupe, GT) *24**, 32
Ajoupa Bouillon (Martinique) *46**, 55
Anse à l'Ane (Martinique) *46**, 59–60
Anse à la Barque (Guadeloupe, BT) *24**, 41
Anse Belleville (Martinique) *46**, 55
Anse Bertrand (Guadeloupe, GT) *24**, 32
Anses-d'Arlets, Les (Martinique) *46**, 60
Arawaks *13, 14, 39*

Baillif (Guadeloupe, BT) *24**, 41
Bananier (Guadeloupe, BT) *24**, 39
Basse-Terre (Guadeloupe) *24**, 25, 33–41*
Basse-Terre (town, Guadeloupe, BT) *24**, 25, 39
Beaches *28, 31, 40, 45, 60, 66, 73–77*
  Anse Céron (Martinique) *46**, 55
  Anse Crawen (Les Saintes) *44*
  Anse des Flamands (St-Barthélemy) *69**, 72
  Anse du Gouverneur (St-Barthélemy) *69**, 72
  Anse de Grande Saline (St-Barthélemy) *69**, 72

Anse Laborde (Guadeloupe, GT) *24**, 32
Anse de Souffleur (Guadeloupe, GT) *24**, 32
Anse Turin (Martinique) *46**, 56
Caravelle (Guadeloupe, GT) *24**, 30
Colombier (St-Barthélemy) *69**, 72
Grande Anse (Guadeloupe, BT) *24**, 35
Pompierre (Les Saintes) *42–44*
St-Jean (St-Barthélemy) *69**, 72
Salines, Les (Martinique) *46**, 60–61
Tarare (Guadeloupe, GT) *24**, 31
Bellefontaine (Martinique) *46**, 56

Capesterre (Guadeloupe, BT) *24**, 37
Caravelle, La (peninsula, Martinique) *46**, 62
Carbet, Le (Martinique) *46**, 56
Carbet, Chutes du (Guadeloupe, BT) *24**, 37–39
Caribs *13–14, 16, 25, 54, 56, 62*
Carnival *89–91*
Cascade aux Ecrevisses (Guadeloupe, BT) *24**, 34
Columbus, Christopher *7, 14, 15, 25, 36–37, 45, 47, 63, 69*

DR JOHNSON'S
Mrs Thrale

DR JOHNSON'S
Mrs Thrale

KATHLEEN DANZIGER

*An imaginary monologue to be read or acted
based on Mrs Thrale's own diaries and
reminiscences of Dr Johnson*

CENTURY PUBLISHING

LONDON

First published in Great Britain in 1984 by
Century Publishing Co. Ltd, Portland House,
12–13 Greek Street, London W1V 5LE

ISBN 0 7126 0920 2

Acknowledgement

'The Months' by Robert Dighton
are Victoria & Albert Museum Crown Copyright
and are reproduced here by permission of
The Witt Library, The Courtauld Institute of Art

Printed in Great Britain by
Butler & Tanner Ltd
Frome and London

For Sonya and Gay

First performed by Gabrielle Hamilton
at the Wolsey Theatre, Ipswich, in March 1984

April

FOREWORD

Mrs Thrale was born in 1741 at Bodvel Hall, near Pwllhelli, in North Wales. Her family, the Salusburys, were impoverished gentlefolk, but family connections saved them from complete disaster and Hester Thrale's mother, Hester Maria Salusbury, was determined to assure her daughter's future through a rich marriage.

This she succeeded in doing, for Hester was married at the age of twenty-two to Henry Thrale, a rich London brewer. Her considerable literary and conversational talents soon attracted the attention of London society and when, through a friend of her husband's, Hester Thrale was introduced to Dr Johnson, a friendship began which ensured her a place in the intellectual life of eighteenth-century London.

Mrs Thrale's marriage had never been a love match. When Henry Thrale died in 1781 she was only forty, and within three years she scandalised London by falling in love with, and marrying, an Italian musician.

At this time, Dr Johnson was ill and nearing the end of his life. Contemporary observers, however, considered that Hester Thrale treated him heartlessly and that her behaviour helped to hasten his death.

Controversy has always surrounded Mrs Thrale's life and reputation. The following short picture of her is an attempt to show her life as she herself might have portrayed it. It is based mainly on her published diary, *Thraliana*, but acknowledgements are also due to the biography by James Clifford.

The character of Hester Thrale seems a fascinating enigma and I hope readers will enjoy this brief portrait.

KATHLEEN DANZIGER

PART ONE

It is eleven o'clock early in January 1821 and Mrs Piozzi, formerly Mrs Thrale, is trying to get together some papers in her writing room. It is a few days before her eightieth birthday.

I am in rather a muddle this morning. I have a young man coming to see me from the *Bath Gazette*. You may think it rather extraordinary that a young man should wish to come and interview an old lady of nearly eighty, but there it is. Because of my birthday party, you see. I rather think it will be my last assembly. If you have any experience of newspaper reporters, you will know that they always ask the most unexpected questions. So I am trying to prepare, but my papers are not at all in order. I have done so much travelling in my life that it has been impossible to keep them as tidy as I would wish.

My daughters complain that there will be far too much for them to go through when I die. I am an authoress, you see, although I fear my work will not survive as long as that of my dear Sam Johnson. Never mind. I am sufficient of a celebrity to be interviewed on the occasion of my eightieth birthday and there are not many people who can say the same. Besides the books I have published, there is my diary. *Thraliana*, I have called it. I certainly would not like extracts of that to be printed in the papers. It was begun on my twenty-fifth birthday, although I made many jottings before then. Then there is my Children's Book and all the letters I have received, besides many I wrote myself. I cannot possibly go through it all this morning, but there may be one or two things to interest this young man. It is most regrettable that nowadays the newspapers are mostly interested in anything which smacks of scandal. They have had a good deal of amusement at my expense, I can tell you. I shall try to avoid that sort of thing this morning. At eighty, one does not wish to expose oneself to scandal and tittle-tattle.

I regret that my early life is of so little interest to the outside world. My childhood was such a happy one, although full of ups and downs on account of my father. He was the first great influence on my life, which is strange considering that I spent so little time with him. He was packed off to the New World, you see. It was the only way for him to avoid his creditors. He went for the first time when I was eight years old after terrible arguments with my mother. She was a gentlewoman and he had brought her to poverty. We were continually packing boxes and living in the houses of relatives. It was cheaper, as you may imagine. I still have the letters my father wrote from the New World. Here is one of the first, written to my dear mama.

> To live an individual, not thought of by anybody, is of all others the most forlorn state. I could have cast aside all ambition for the happiness of being always with thee, but alas, we were not able to live up to our rank. God bless thee, my dear life. Take care of thyself and the dear little girl. I am out of the reach of sneers and insults and fairly practice every honest endeavour to gain an independency. The twenty-ninth of May, 1749, no happy day to me nor any other absent from my dear love.

The reporter will not be interested in that. But to read these old letters brings back such memories. My father came and went twice from Nova Scotia, a place I am glad to say I have never had the misfortune to visit. But meanwhile, I was growing up. Thanks to my mother's more affluent relatives, I learned languages from my tutor. I also had dancing lessons and went to the theatre. At my grandmother's I learned to drive from the old coachman, but this met with extreme disfavour. I always loved horses and riding, of which my mother and Henry Thrale continually disapproved.

My mother and Henry Thrale! There was an alliance to conjure with! I have said that my father was the first great influence on my life, but it was my mother who determined my fate.

Now, let me see, what is there here which could possibly interest the *Bath Gazette*? I should very much like them to publish one of my poems. All they ever do is to publish anecdotes about me and Dr Johnson. They do not seem to realise that I had a life before the good doctor.

I have a poem here that I wrote when I was seventeen. I would like your opinion on it.

> The setting sun declared the close of day,
> And Philomela tuned her parting lay.
> The dew began to drop, the owl t'affright,
> And evening objects grew upon the sight.
> The winds were still and nature seemed inclined
> To sooth the sadness of a troubled mind.

I don't think they are likely to publish it, do you? But it is no worse than much of Thomas Gray's and certainly no worse than that of a certain Mr Marriot.

Just when my mother began her fateful encounter with Henry Thrale, we were staying at Offley Park, which was the home of my father's elder brother. He had had the luck to marry an heiress. Like my father, he had been penniless before his marriage and had the reputation of an idler and a gambler. But the heiress he had the good fortune to marry was ageing and an epileptic. My uncle exerted himself to court her. He dwelt on her accomplishments of mind and her beauty of spirit, which was ingenious of him, for there was little enough to dwell on. And what has all this to do with poetry and Mr Thrale and Mr Marriot? I will tell you.

My uncle's wife seemed unlikely to bear children, so my mother hastened to Offley Park with me, her seventeen-year-old daughter. My uncle was quickly disposed to love me and I truly think my mother and I brightened his life. We had many visitors and Mr Marriot and Henry Thrale were among them. Mr Thrale was a brewer and Mr Marriot was a poet. Now, which in all conscience would a young girl prefer? Mr Marriot and I discussed his newly published verses. The critics called him an indifferent rhymester, but to me publication was glory in itself. 'I would be proud to have my verses published, whatever the opinion of the critics,' I said to Mr Marriot.

'But you will be published, Miss Salusbury,' he replied. 'You will be the great poetess of our age.' We recited our poems and talked for hours at a time and in fact Mr Marriot became quite a suitor. I did indeed fancy myself as a poetess and I longed to make my way by writing. What a stupid young girl I was. In my day it was marriage only that secured a young girl's fortune. That and the hope of a good inheritance of course. So there I was with a good chance of inheriting Offley Park and no wonder my mother looked with disfavour on a penniless if romantic young poet. My father, returning from Nova Scotia, became acquainted with the situation and wrote Mr Marriot a furious letter.

Sir,
My daughter shewed me an extraordinary letter from you. She resents the ill-treatment as conscious that she never gave any pretence to take such liberties with her. I think it hard that insolence and impudence should be suffered to interrupt the tranquil state of youth and innocence. I therefore insist on no altercations – no more trash on the subject. Should you continue to insult my poor child, I do assume the father. I will be avenged on you much to the detriment of your person and – so help me God – John Salusbury.

My poor father. It was hard for him to accept that his
darling little girl was at an age for suitors. He soon had
a far more formidable adversary - my mother - and in
alliance with her, Henry Thrale.

The newspapers have said many unkind things about
me and one of them is that I never truly loved my first
husband. What a very unkind conjecture! The anniversary
of our marriage never returns without bringing many a
tender remembrance. We lived seventeen years together
in perfect amity and I had twelve children by nearly the
handsomest man in England. I have his picture here. 'Tis
true he grew a trifle portly, but more of that later. I wish
to make it clear to this reporter what a very wise choice
my Mama made for me. Of course I shall not tell him
that in the beginning it was a match of mere prudence
and common good liking without the smallest pretension
to passion on either side. It was on the day we married,
when we retired together that I was first alone with Mr
Thrale for five minutes in my whole life.

But I am rushing on too fast. Rattling on, Dr Johnson
would have said. He called me his rattle. You may wonder why Mr Thrale, the owner of a brewery to rival Mr
Whitbread's, a city business man of wealth and position,
should be interested in a silly little poetess with a penniless
father. There were two winning cards which my mother
held in her hand, Offley Park and my pedigree. I have
not yet told you that I am Welsh. Many people are surprised to hear it. I am descended, on the wrong side of
the blanket, from Henry VII through the Cloughs, the
Wynns, the Thelwalls and the Salusburys, all renowned

Welsh families. Henry Thrale had no such pedigree and was anxious to acquire one. Alas, although he was to acquire my lineage, Mr Thrale never acquired Offley Park. My epileptic aunt died prematurely and my uncle married a rich widow.

My parents and I were staying in London when a note came from my tutor to say that my uncle would certainly marry the widow the Sunday following. He begged I would not say a syllable and he would come the next day and break the dreadful tidings to my father.

Alas, my father thought the note was from Henry Thrale! He accused me of receiving clandestine letters. I of course denied it, and after many hours of fruitless contest I fainted. My father thereupon gained possession of the fatal billet. He had to ask my pardon, poor unhappy fellow, and we spent several hours in shared misery. At length I was sent to call to dinner our medical friend, Dr Lawrence, for by this time we were all ill. But by the time he came, my father had died. He was a corpse before the dining hour. He was fifty-five and this happened sixty years ago, yet are not my feelings blunted.

My uncle got me off his conscience with a settlement of £10,000 and this satisfied Mr Thrale, for we were married.

Everyone knows about Streatham Park, the house to which Mr Thrale brought me. I know very well that this young man will ask me about our famous dinner parties – Mr Thrale was a great gourmet – and about Sir Joshua Reynolds and Dr Goldsmith and Mr Burke and all the famous people who visited us there, not to mention the doctor. I have all his sayings here in one of my books. I can reel them off by heart, so many times have I been asked about them. But no one is ever interested in the young girl, not in love but a bride, the mistress of a great house and yet its prisoner, who first came to Streatham Park. Not only to Streatham Park but to Southwark, the dark house near the brewery where we passed our first winters. It was in Deadman's Place. Is that not a name to terrify a young girl? And to me it was Deadman's Place, dead to society, dead to the fashionable side of London, dead to culture, to everything I held most dear. The first years of my marriage were interminably long, with my husband away at the brewery – or at the brothel – while I sat in the parlour with my mother or wrote at my writing desk.

But life moves on, fortunately or unfortunately. Here is an entry in my diary, *Thraliana*, which marks the great turning point in my life with Henry Thrale: 'It was on the second Thursday of the month of January 1765, that I first saw Mr Johnson in a room.' The reporters always like that. 'How?' they ask. 'Why?' they ask. Well, it was on account of my husband's friendship with an Irish dramatist called Arthur Murphy who was a friend of Sam Johnson also. It was he who persuaded the doctor to visit us and so to him I owe the friendship which transformed our marriage.

Mr Murphy had prepared me somewhat for Dr Johnson's appearance, but it was something of a shock nevertheless. That his face was disfigured by the scrofula is too well-known to mention. His partial deafness and half blindness from the same disease were other impediments. His height was five foot eleven inches without shoes, his neck short, his bones large and his shoulders broad. His hands were handsome in spite of dirt and such deformity as perpetual picking of the fingers produces. His leg, too, was eminently handsome. When he first came to us at Streatham Park, his clothes were a disgrace and his wigs filthy. I have often been criticised for dwelling on these shortcomings of the doctor, but the public seem pleased enough to read about them nevertheless.

By then, I had had my first child – a daughter. She was christened Hester Maria, but soon became known to us all as Queeney, for Sam Johnson called her the queen of his heart. It was then that I began my Children's Book; I have a copy here now, under this pile of papers. The doctor encouraged me in all my writings. He is often said to be the enemy of our sex, but this is not the case. A friend of ours consulted him once as to whether he should educate his daughters. 'To be sure,' said he. 'Let them learn all they can. It is a paltry trick indeed to deny women the cultivation of their mental powers, and I think it is partly a proof that we are afraid of them that we endeavour to keep them un-armed.' So here is my first entry:

My daughter can walk and run alone up and down all smooth places even if pretty steep. Although the back string is still kept on, it is no longer of use. She is strong enough to carry a hound puppy quite across the lawn. Also, she can carry a bowl such as are used on bowling greens. She is eminently pretty and can repeat most words plain enough.

She repeats Our Father and knows her letters great and small. She knows her figures and the simplest combinations of them and all the heathen deities and their attributes without missing one.

At this time, Queeney was two years old.

Queeney. She is here at this minute, helping me to prepare for my birthday party. What a part she has played in my life. I have been much criticised for the treatment of my children, but ye Gods, how they have treated me!

But this is not what I wish to tell the young man. It is the pleasanter side of our life at Streatham Park that I shall dwell on.

The house itself was six miles from London and faced directly on Tooting Upper Common. A sweeping drive led from the lodge gate to a house surrounded by a park of a hundred acres. At the back were farm buildings, domestic offices, greenhouses, stables and an ice house. Behind these were kitchen gardens, with forcing frames for grapes, melons, peaches and nectarines. Mr Thrale himself supervised these. He was a great trencherman and in the early days of our marriage, I was allowed no say in the choice of food. Truly, I never knew what was to come to table until it arrived.

It was a comfortable country mansion. Later, as our income increased, we added a library, a summerhouse, lawns and so on. Streatham Park was the focus of my life with Henry Thrale and indeed of my life with Dr Johnson.

I suppose we were a very strange combination. At dinner on any evening I was likely to be the hostess to a crowd of witty gentlemen, perhaps Mr Boswell, Sam Johnson himself, Dr Goldsmith and Sir Joshua Reynolds. Little Dr Goldsmith was continually enraged that Johnson could never be worsted in an argument. He spoke very shrilly thus:

'Why am I always to be put down and continually out-argued at your dinner-table, madam? No one will dispute that I am the better writer than Johnson. None will dispute that my works are more popular, that my drama plays better, that in all respects I am the superior hack. Yet that great mountain of a man, that pontificator slobbering into his chocolate, that haunch of venison out-argues and out-guns me. It is ... outrageous.'

Even in my partial judgment, it is undoubtedly true that Goldsmith's writings are of a quality to outlast Dr Johnson's, but my dear doctor's superiority as a man is in no question.

I myself was no passive spectator at these dinner parties, I can tell you. I flatter myself that if Henry Thrale presided over the menu, I presided over the conversation. I did not gain my reputation as a raconteuse for nothing. Perhaps one day there will even be a little book: 'The sayings of Mrs Thrale.' I shall mention this to the reporter. My husband did not converse very much. Indeed, he was known as the silent Thrale. There was a series of great shocks in his life which contributed to this effect and the first one was the occasion on which he faced bankruptcy.

Oh, yes, people think that I have never been poor, but it was not only in childhood that I stared poverty in the face. Mr Thrale was not as good a business man as every-one imagined and quite early in our marriage he was nearly ruined by a scoundrel called Jackson.

He came in late to dinner one evening, smelling of drink. This in itself was unusual, for he was a temperate man. It was June 1772. The city was in any case in a panic, for one of the banking houses had failed and busi-ness after business had collapsed. 'I am undone, madam,' he cried. 'I have no beer to sell for this year's supply.' Apparently, this Jackson had persuaded him to a new method of brewing which had totally failed. I organised a conference immediately, while Mr Thrale behaved as if he were paralysed. I flew to Dr Johnson, my mother was called in and together we set about raising money.

Our chief clerk was a man named Mr Perkins and he became a great help to me, for I had never concerned myself with the business before. I found I really did better with the work-people than poor Mr Thrale – and as for Dr Johnson, he learned to judge the price of malt and to take an interest in the harvest of wheat. I think he really enjoyed it. The brewery was saved, although deep in debt for several years. The heaviest price was the death of a little daughter, born the September following. She lived but ten hours. Henry Thrale sat at home for most of that summer and none of us could rouse him. He had been saved by a scholar and a parcel of women and he never quite recovered from the shock.

By this time, the doctor was in the habit of staying with us quite regularly. He had his particular room both at Southwark and at Streatham Park. My master had a very good effect on him. He saw to it that Dr Johnson's clothes were clean and in order, that he put silver buckles on his shoes and that he changed more often than formerly. On occasion, a servant stood outside the dining-room with a fresh wig, for the doctor's habit of reading too close to the candle singed his wigs most severely.

The newspapers, of course, did not allow Dr Johnson's constant presence at our house to go unremarked. The *Westminster Magazine* had a column called 'The Court of Cupid.' You can imagine what scandal they delighted to publish there! There was a famous courtesan at that time in London called Polly Hart. After all our troubles with the brewery, you can imagine my feelings when I read in the *Westminster Magazine* that she was the recipient of Mr Thrale's diamonds. Diamonds, indeed! Why should Polly Hart receive diamonds while I struggled with the counting-house clerks? The magazine reported that Polly had fallen into the arms of a Borough brewer more famous for his amours than for his beer. She soon tired of him, however. One lover is seldom enough for such ladies as Mrs Hart.

For his part, Mr Thrale was by no means pleased when the following item appeared: '... that an eminent brewer was very jealous of a certain author in folio and perceived a strong resemblance to him in his eldest son.'

Here is an entry in my Children's Book which records his birth: 'February 15th, 1767. I was delivered of a healthy son who thank God seems likely to live. He is to be named Henry Salusbury.'

Although Queeney was a lively and intelligent child

and I was very proud of her, she was strangely cold and lacking in affection. But my little Harry was a darling. He gave me all the affection which Queeney did not, and as he grew older he and I and Queeney and Dr Johnson made a fine quartet together. As to the newspaper's slur on his birth, I can tell you it was a nonsense. Dr Johnson was at that time nearly sixty. To me, he became father, confidant and friend. Whatever the newspapers may say, love and friendship are distinct things and I would go through fire for many a man whom nothing less than fire would force me to go to bed with.

And his feelings for me? He was a man of great religious feeling. His wife was dead, and unlike Mr Thrale I do believe he considered any fornication outside marriage to be a mortal sin. He wrote, 'That I certainly do love you better than any human being I ever saw.' Yet such was his respect for my master – and although I often sat far into the night drinking tea with him, for he was a bad sleeper, poor man – he never prevailed on me for his carnal appetite. Indeed, he would have preferred me to whip him at his bed-post rather than to satisfy such longings. Poor Sam.

But I was talking of Harry:

23rd of March, 1776. On his ninth birthday, we had a party for him at Streatham Park. A few weeks after that, a visitor of my husband's being with us, we planned a visit to the Tower. All went well. We went first to see a ship in the river, bound for Boston with our beer aboard. Then we went to see the lions and the artillery, and Harry got into every mortar until he was as black as the ground. Later, we

May

June

July

August

also went to Brooke's menagerie, where I sought advice about one of my pea-fowl. Harry was interested in a lion intended for a show that was remarkably tame and a monkey that was so beautiful and gentle that it pleased me as much as it pleased the children. Here we met a Mr Hervey who took notice of the boy, how well he looked. 'Yes,' I said, 'if the dirt was scraped off him.'

Next morning he had breakfasted, as he loved to do, with the clerks at the brew-house. He returned with two penny cakes for Queeney, and made her dance a minuet for them, for he loved to tease her. Poor Queeney, she could never dance. That same morning, he began to complain of a sudden severe pain in his right side. He was sick and when his countenance began to alter, I sent for a physician. As soon as he came, he gave Harry an emetic. He poulticed him and tried a hot bath. When Mr Thrale returned from the city, he bid me not cry so, for he did not apprehend the danger which I felt. I had never seen my brave Harry so distressed. By the afternoon, the pain appeared unbearable. But then, even worse, his whimpers began to subside. His writhings grew less and my bright Harry of the morning ... was dead. Something died in me, also. I forced myself never again to love a child so deeply.

The effect on Mr Thrale was frightening. He sat on an arm-chair in the corner of the room, both hands in his waistcoat pockets, with his body so stiffly erect, and with such a ghastly smile on his face, that it was quite horrid to behold. As long as I live, I shall never forget that smile. My maid told me afterwards that I fainted three times, but I do not remember.

Later that year, Harry's little pet dog also died. Queeney asked for him to be buried under a little pippin tree which her brother had planted. She asked me for an epitaph and I gave her these four lines.

> This pippin tree poor Harry planted,
> Which once supplied him all he wanted,
> And now affords both shade and rest to
> His little favourite faithful Presto.

Dr Johnson was away in Lichfield at the time of Harry's death. I have the letter here which he wrote me:

My dear Mistress,
I am conscious of your great grief and I am concerned that it will drive you into solitary ways. Remember the great precept. Be not solitary. Be not idle. Keep yourself busy and you will in time grow cheerful.

How many times in my life did I have cause to remember those words! As to keeping busy, that was scarcely a problem with Mr Thrale's household to run. I remember that soon after that, Queeney was troubled by worms. I found tin pills a most successful remedy, although my doctor did not approve of them and I am ashamed to say we quarrelled violently. I always purged the servants with tin pills twice a year, and no harm resulted that I saw ever.

Harry's death was the second great shock to my poor husband within the space of a few years. To lose a son and so nearly to lose a great business were trials which, I am sure, combined to undermine his health. He sought comfort in ways which did not help, either. I need hardly say that there were other successors to Mrs Hart. That and his eating. 'What can be done with a man,' Dr Johnson would cry, 'whose mouth cannot be sewed up?' Yet Dr Johnson himself ate voraciously. I have recorded in my diary his notion of a good dinner.

A leg of pork boiled 'til it drops from the bone almost: a veal pie with plums and sugar and the outside of a buttock of beef. Next a pudding sauced with melted butter, followed by mountains of fruit. He loved fruit exceedingly and though I have seen him eat of it immensely, he said he never had his belly full of it but once at our house. When he left off drinking wine he made up for it by drinking chocolate liberally and putting in it large quantities of butter or cream.

Mr Boswell often tried to provoke him on the subject of wine:

'I cannot think, sir, why you reject a harmless glass. It is a balm to the spirit and a spur to the conversation.'

'I know of no good that it does whatsoever,' the doctor would reply.

'But sir,' maintained Mr Boswell, 'it makes a man eloquent.'

'I think, sir, it makes a man noisy and absurd.'

'This you must allow, it makes a man speak truth.'

'I see no good there is in that neither, sir, unless he is a liar when he is sober.'

In the biography I wrote of Johnson, I was much criticised for putting in anecdotes which might seem to detract from the doctor's great reputation. The press were quick enough to publish them, however.

I remember a visit which we made to the home of Fanny Burney's father, Dr Burney. Fanny was at the time all the rage becausse of her new novel, *Evelina*. We had gathered to hear Dr Johnson talk, but alas he was wrapped in his own thoughts and would not. Perhaps it was because he was better dressed than usual. He was wearing a new wig, which may have irritated him. Whatever the matter, any new sally from any of us remained disregarded until we were all in despair.

Then an incident occurred which ever afterwards filled me with shame. A Signor Piozzi was introduced. He was a handsome Italian who was a singer and teacher of music; a composer too, as I later discovered. On this occasion, Dr Burney asked him to perform in an attempt to lighten our spirits. We had already been bored half to death by some duets from Dr Burney's younger children, so he faced an audience half-asleep. He was halfway through some sentimental ditty or other, with everyone yawning, when the temptation to liven up the proceedings overcame me. Stealing behind poor young Signor Piozzi, I began to imitate his gestures. The audience livened considerably, so that the Signor redoubled his efforts as the interest increased. I was greatly enjoying the pantomime and so, I believe, were my audience when I noticed Mr Thrale begin to swell and redden with rage.

He began to gesticulate in a most unseemly manner, which made matters worse, for Signor Piozzi concluded that his singing was the reason for my master's displeasure and faltered to a stop. That was the end of the evening. Even my rattling tongue was quiet. Mr Thrale and I, to my regret, had high words in the coach on the way home.

You can see now why I never intend to allow my diary to be published. There has been much written on the subject of myself and Signor Piozzi, but nothing about our first meeting, I am glad to say. It was some time before we met again – by accident in a bookseller's in Brighton.

Where was I? I declare, the older I get, the more my mind runs on this and that until I am quite bewildered.

I really must look up these sayings of Dr Johnson. I have them here under subjects. On the passion of love. 'No person, madam, ever yet treated love with contempt except from stupidity or disappointment. Those who were never in love never were happy, for nature will vindicate her own feelings and revenge the insults offered her.'

So were you happy, doctor, under my roof, loving me and yet so far from fulfilment? I think you were happier than you ever were before. Those who criticise me forget that in my household you passed your most prosperous and your most contented days.

Like me, you had known poverty and pitied it in others. 'The loss of a parent, child or friend,' you used to say, 'are distresses of sentiment which a man really to be pitied has no leisure to feel. The want of food and raiment is so common in London that one who lives there has no compassion to spare for the wounds given only to vanity or softness.'

Dr Johnson was commonly struck by the vacuity of life. If a man was profligate, followed the girls or gaming table: 'Why, life must be filled up, madam,' he would say, 'and the man was capable of nothing less sensual.'

Another man was active in the management of his estate and delighted in domestic economy. 'Why a man must do something, and what so easy to a narrow mind as hoarding half-pence until they turn into silver?' I thought there might be a little of envy in that remark, for the doctor loved well enough to interest himself in the affairs of the brewery. But nowadays one must not say a word against a national monument like Dr Johnson. And as for Mrs Thrale to have the temerity to criticise him, well...!

How can I possibly make this young man from the *Bath Gazette* understand the brilliance of our life in London? Here is a note from my diary of 1777, at the time of my presentation at Court: 'The ceremony was trifling but I am glad it is done. One is now upon the footing one wishes to be and in a manner, free of the drawing-rooms of London. I confess I am pleased to have been there.'

Soon after, I dined with Mrs Montague and a duchess desired leave to visit me. The King himself said I spent too little time in London because I lived too near it. Dazzling days!

Here is an entry about a visit with Dr Johnson to the studio of a sculptor called Nollekens:

who said to Dr Johnson, 'I like the portrait of you by Sir

Joshua very much. I hear it is for Thrale, a brewer over the water. His wife's a sharp woman, one of the blue-stocking people.'

'Nolly, Nolly,' observed the doctor, 'I wish you would stop your foolish mouth with a blue bag.' At which I smiled and whispered to the doctor, 'My dear sir, you'll get nothing by blunting your arrows upon a block.'

Dr Johnson was mine, my conquest, and because of him all London beat a path to my door – the brewer's wife. However scandalmongers chose to gossip, he was the crown of my life with Henry Thrale. For my sake, he concerned himself with the business of the brewery. For my sake, he composed election addresses for Mr Thrale when he stood as the member for Southwark. For my sake, he played with the children and comforted them.

This is a tribute I wrote to him when all London admired him and envied him. I was known then as 'Dr Johnson's Mrs Thrale'.

Swelling with envy see some wretch appears,
While hourly quoted Ramblers grieve his ears,
Swelling with envy, eyes the crowded park,
Where shrugs significant my person mark.
Swelling with envy, sees one pension paid
To conscious worth that scorns the flattering trade.
Swelling with envy, sees the calm retreat
That Streatham's shades afford his weary feet.
Swelling with envy, hears the meaner fame
That Johnson's court to Johnson owes its name.

Swelling with envy, sees each friend I love,
Pleas'd while corrected and while check'd, approved.
Swelling with envy which affords no power
To damp the pleasures of my social hour.
See how with envy swelled and spleen accurst,
But if he swells with envy – let him burst!

PART TWO

Queeney has just been in to say that I made a mistake about the young man from the *Bath Gazette*. He is not to come today but tomorrow. I made a mistake, indeed! Queeney is trying to suggest that my brain is addled with old age. She made the appointment, and I can assure you it was she who made the mistake. My memory is as clear as ever it was, but my daughters have always delighted in trying to demean me. They have been a great trial to me, all of them. Ever since Mr Thrale's death, my family has been set against me. I have tried to be a good mother, but all for naught, it seems. Queeney has a title now. She is Lady Keith, if you please. She waited long enough for it, forty-four before she married and then to an old widower. But her temperament was always cold, so it suited her well enough. She is clucking with disapproval over my birthday party. Says I cannot afford it. It is none of her business whether I can afford it or not. She was well enough provided for by her father in all conscience. There is to be a concert, a ball and a supper for six hundred people. Well, you know how it is. Once you start to make a list, there are so many people you cannot leave out!

I am happy to say that society accepts me again, just as in the days of dear Dr Johnson. But after Mr Thrale's death, I had a struggle, I can tell you. Once one becomes a widow, the whole world begins to enquire as to whether one means to marry again.

As soon as I have finished my tea, I must get on with sorting my papers. Queeney says that the litter I make is quite impossible. Well, as soon as my party is over she can leave me and my litter and go back to London. She never did like parties. The truth is, as I said before, she dances incomparably ill. Before Mr Thrale's death, when we were at Brighton, people used to twit me that I would not let Queeney dance because I danced myself. But the truth was that she cut a very poor figure and knew it. I have always been complimented on my dancing. Indeed, I shall lead it off at my birthday party. Here is an entry in my diary that the Bath newspapers will be interested in. It concerns the riots in Bath, in 1781.

I was staying in Pulteney St. with my dear Fanny Burney, when we first had news of the riots in London. A bill had been introduced in Parliament to improve the position of Roman Catholic priests and a fanatical man called Lord Gordon was stirring up opposition to it. All who were reputed to be Catholics were in danger and feeling rapidly spread all over the country. One evening rioters set fire to the Roman Catholic chapel in Bath. I am ashamed to say that Fanny and I were standing at a window enjoying the spectacle when my maid came rushing into the room. 'Lor, ma'am,' she gasped, 'the rumour is in Bath that you and Mr

Thrale are Catholics and that the mob may make their way here this very night.'

Fanny burst into tears but I had no time to cry. We did not wait to see if the rumour was true. I gave orders for the horses to be harnessed immediately and we packed our bags and left Bath that very night.

At Brighton, the news was even worse. Mr Thrale had had word that a London mob had attempted to storm the brewery.

You may well ask why Mr Thrale had not set off immediately for London. I will come to that in a moment. At any event, it was I who set out with all speed for Southwark. My dear Dr Johnson speedily joined me and we went to view the precipice we had just escaped. The mob had actually forced their way into the brewhouse and in a few minutes would probably have burnt it to the ground. Perkins, however, with rare presence of mind, plied the crowd with meat and drink and I am told the whole thing turned into a party.

We owe the saving of our fortune to our chief clerk. He became an important figure in our lives from then on. I gave two hundred guineas to Mr Perkins for his loyalty and bravery, and to his wife I presented a silver urn.

But to get back to Mr Thrale and why he had not rushed off to London. Truth to tell, Mr Thrale was in love. That I shall certainly not tell the *Bath Gazette*. I am not talking about a whorehouse hussy either, but a lady well respected in society, a Miss Sophia Streatfield. It was in Brighton that Mr Thrale and I first met her. This was at our house in West St. where we went most summers, I to bathe and Mr Thrale to hunt. At first I was enchanted, for she was the pupil of my own dear old tutor, Dr Collier. Her scholarship was well-known, and her beauty too, although to me it was somewhat anaemic and pale, like a white fricassée might appear alongside a plate of good red beef. One talent she had which was most extraordinary – she could fill her eyes with tears at any desired moment.

'Yes, do cry a little, Sophie, pray do,' I would say to entertain the company and sure enough a tear would well up and fall down her cheek. One evening at the end of a *conversazione*, when Miss Streatfield had positively hung about my master with soft, insinuating glances and sly squeezes of the hand at parting, I ventured to bring up the subject. 'Do you not think, Mr Thrale,' I said, 'that Miss Streatfield's dress of pale green satin goes rather ill with her pallid complexion?'

'I did not notice the colour of her dress,' replied my master. 'I seldom notice which colour a lady is wearing on any particular day.' 'Perhaps you were too concerned with gazing into her eyes,' said I. Mr Thrale responded with unusual vigour, 'When it comes to eye-gazing, madam, you and Signor Piozzi are seldom to be surpassed.' It is true my stay in Brighton had been somewhat enlivened by the Italian musician. He appeared not to remember the unfortunate evening at Dr Burney's. Queeney and I first met him at the bookseller's shop where he played on a public instrument every morning. His hand on the piano was so soft, so sweet, so delicate.

Every tone went to one's heart, filling the mind with emotions one would not be without, though inconvenient enough sometimes.

But I was talking about Miss Streatfield. She had a house in London in Clifford Square and when Parliament called Mr Thrale to London, he found it convenient to spend his evenings there. I am told he left his carriage round the corner at his sister's, so that Sophie's reputation might not be damaged. Queeney knows nothing of this, of course, let alone the younger girls who were children at the time. But even if she did know, I doubt if it would alter by one iota her opinion of her father and her opinion of me. Mr Thrale, with his ladies of ill-repute and his fashionable mistress, was still held high in the opinion of London society. In this, even Dr Johnson supported my master against me. Whereas I who had lived so blamelessly was instantly pilloried because I failed to marry the man society had chosen for me after Mr Thrale died.

The winter he died – what a winter that was! We rented a fashionable house in Grosvenor Square. It was as if Mr Thrale knew that his final hour awaited him and wished to put aside the knowledge with continuous gaiety. Our dining hour was moved from three to eight in accordance with the upper circles of society and the procession to our table of famous and witty people never ceased. It was small wonder, since our dinners were famous. Twenty-one dishes at each course, desserts of fruit, ices and creams. Mr Thrale could not be kept from eating, although as his health grew worse his physicians constantly warned him against full meals. My dear Piozzi

was a constant visitor. So was Miss Sophia Streatfield.
Mrs Montague and I often talked to entertain the company. Here is what I have put in my diary:

> Mrs Montague and I meet somewhere every night. People
> think they must not ask one of us without the other. Some-
> times Mrs Montague will harangue the company on her
> own, but when there is no music we talk away regularly.
> The folks look so stupid – except one or two who I have a
> notion, lie by to laugh – and write letters home to their
> sisters about us.

It was Queeney who found her father lying on the
floor of his chamber one evening after an enormous dinner. 'What's the meaning of this?' she said. 'I chuse it,'
replied my master firmly. 'I lie so o' purpose.' A messen-
ger was sent for Dr Pepys, but before he arrived Mr
Thrale had suffered an attack of apoplexy. There followed
another and another. I could not bear the preparations for
bleeding and went to my room. Dear Dr Johnson, he sat
all night with my master. I was generous enough to send
for Sophia Streatfield, but she was out of town and could
not come. Dr Johnson wrote later:

> On Sunday, 1st April, Thrale's physician warned him of
> his diet. On Monday, I pressed him to observance of his
> rules, but without effect. Tuesday I was absent, but his wife
> pressed forbearance on him, again unsuccessfully. At night
> I was called to his room and found him senseless, in strong
> convulsions. I staid in the room except that I visited Mrs
> Thrale twice. About five on Wednesday morning, he ex-
> pired. I felt almost the last flutter of his pulse, and looked
> for the last time on the face that for fifteen years had never
> been turned on me but with respect and benignity.

What a blessing that in our day women were not expected to attend funerals. Dr Johnson saw to the burial and Queeney and I fled to Brighton. My children were now fatherless. Of the twelve children I bore to nearly the handsomest man in England, only five were living, all girls. And they all preferred their father to me. After all, it is easy to love the image of a dead parent – far easier than to love a living one. Yet my own mother and I were so close. They never forgave my second marriage, that was it. As if it was the smallest hurt or consequence to them.

Queeney and I did not remain long in Brighton, for there was too much to do. First of all, there was the brew-house to manage. If an angel from heaven had told me twenty years before that the man known as 'Dictionary Johnson' should one day become partner with me in a great trade, that we should jointly and severally sign notes or drafts of three or four thousand pounds of a morning, how unlikely it would have seemed ever to happen. Unlikely is no word though, it would have seemed incredible. A few years before, neither of us was worth a groat and both of us were far removed from commerce. Dr Johnson, however, seemed delighted to see his name in a new character, flaming away at the bottom of bonds and leases. He was overjoyed with his new employment as a merchant.

Mrs Montague said I should have a statue erected to me for my diligent attendance on my counting-house duties. What else could I have done, though, to ensure the inheritance of my girls? Small thanks I got. When did

Dr Johnson's Mrs Thrale

a mother ever get thanks from her children? She is foolish to expect it. I soon grew anxious to sell the brewery and my manager, Perkins, was only too anxious to acquire it. He was fast on the way to becoming a gentleman and now occupied our old house in Deadman's Place. Well, I always hated it. Queeney was born there. I think the place got into her soul, somehow. I was only too happy to let Perkins purchase it.

He had insufficient capital, however, so a Mr Barclay came in. A Lombard St. banker – need I say more? Then there was Mr Crutchley. And who was Mr Crutchley, you may ask? You may well ask. He was rumoured to be Mr Thrale's natural son, although whether he was or no I cannot say as I was naturally not privy to the circumstances. He was very partial to Queeney, a circumstance that needed careful watching, I can tell you. I can well imagine how they plotted the purchase of my brewery!

Perkins with his cockney voice: 'Now, Mr Crutchley,' I can hear him saying, 'you are with Mrs Thrale a great deal. Friendly with the eldest Miss Thrale, I 'ear. D'yer think she's in a selling mood?'

'No doubt of it,' Crutchley would reply, brushing some dust off his coat. He had that brushing habit like the fops in Bond St.

'Only that great fellow Johnson likes the position of influence it gives him. Being her co-executor, you know. If she does as is rumoured and marries him, then she won't sell, I'll be bound.'

'And will she marry Dr Johnson?' asked Mr Barclay in measured tones.

September

November

December

'The world says so,' confided Crutchley, 'but I do not say so.' More brushing, and a touch to the side of the nose and a wink. Perkins is all curiosity.

'Got another fella in mind, then, 'as she? A woman of that fortune will 'ave fellas in plenty, though she is on the wrong side of forty.'

Crutchley becomes confidential. 'There's a very nice little foursome at Streatham,' he says. 'Miss Thrale and I are very companionable together, although I could never, you know ... the circumstances of my birth ...'

'Hrrrrrhum,' would go the other two gentlemen. 'The other couple is the mistress – and a certain musical gentleman.'

'Ah, Signor Powsy,' cries Perkins, 'but she'll never marry 'im. A pleasant gentleman, but too far down in the world.'

'That's what the town thinks, but I think differently,' responded Crutchley. 'A rich woman past middle age and deep in love will do as she pleases.'

Mr Barclay would have come in here. 'This Signor – Powsy?'

'Piozzi,' corrected Crutchley.

'Do I gather he is a musical gentleman?' Mr Barclay went on.

' 'E sings,' replied Perkins.

'Well, then, not a man of business?'

'Business? Lord luv yer, the sweet gentleman wouldn't know a business contract from one of 'is musical scores. Never 'ad two lira to rub together. Why, the mistress pays all 'is tailor's bills, I'll be bound.'

Mr Barclay would have been very cheerful at this. 'If your suppositions are correct, Mr Crutchley, then the brewery is as good as ours. Signor Piozzi will hardly wish his new wife to be dancing attendance at the counting-house.'

'Nothin' against the gentleman, but my 'eart is sad for poor old Sam Johnson. Why, they say that to marry Mrs Thrale, Sam would throw off his bush wig, wear a clean shirt an' shave every day, give up snuff, learn to eat vermicelli and leave off red flannel night-caps.'

Perkins had grown fond of Dr Johnson. They got on well together.

'I will help you two gentlemen to the brewery if I can,' Mr Crutchley told them, 'but only if the price is fair. For myself, I cannot come in. Unfortunately, I have no money. The position of an illegitimate son, you know.'

'But we shall commission you, sir,' Mr Barclay promised. 'If you smooth our path, you shall not be the loser.'

So the gentlemen talked and eventually approached me. A bargain was struck and the business sold for £135,000. Farewell, brewhouse and Deadman's Place! Adieu to trade and frigid tradesmen. Good luck to you, Mr Barclay and Mr Perkins, and may your brewery prosper. I have lost the golden mill-stone from around my neck. I salute you in my restored character of a gentle-woman!

I knew nothing when I wrote about that in my diary, nothing! Until that moment, my life had been all upwards. Oh yes, I had had my tragedies. The deaths of my dear babies, my troubles with Mr Thrale. But in the eyes of London society, in the eyes of the town, I rode high like a ship in full sail. My ship was riding into stormy water and I stood at the helm, smiling like a fool.

I have it all here, newspaper cuttings, letters. I kept a record of it all. I have no doubt that when I die, and that cannot be far off, Queeney will make a bonfire of it all. What the newspapers said about me angered her more than me. It was not the slights on my reputation, it was the risk to her future standing in society that worried her. And what was the crime society accused me of? That I was in love.

The truth was that society wished me to marry Dr Johnson. The *Morning Star* even announced that a treaty of marriage was on tap between us. I never troubled to deny such nonsense and I must admit, I never gave thought to the pain it must be causing my poor old Sam. He was not well at this time in any case – but must I, a woman in the prime of life, saddle myself with yet more illness and invalids? I had had enough, I can tell you.

The object of my affections was also in the prime of life, was handsome, was cultured, was all the things a woman of sensitivity could admire. My sweet Piozzi! He plunged me into disgrace, but it was worth it. As soon as the newspapers discovered how the land lay, it began. Here is a verse that appeared in the *Morning Herald*.

Most writers agree and I know it a truth,
We all love a frolic in days of our youth,
But what shall we say when such grave ones engage
And frolic in love in the days of old age?

Old age, indeed! Who thinks of forty as 'old age'? And why all this fuss? Because the town said my lover was below me. In what was he below me? In virtue? I wish I had been above him. In understanding? Mine was henceforth under the guardianship of his. Yes, he was below me in birth, but so was almost every man I knew or had a chance to know. He was below me in fortune, but mine was sufficient for us both. How could any man deserve fortune if *he* did not? He had the spirit of a gentleman with the talents of a professor. But I was the guardian of five daughters by Mr Thrale and could not disgrace their name and family. Was their father of higher extraction than Signor Piozzi? No, but his fortune was higher. I needed fortune when I married Mr Thrale, but as a wealthy widow I no longer needed it. Might I not please myself at last? I married the first time to please my mother, and it seemed that the second time I must marry to please my daughters.

That little traitress, Fanny Burney, wrote this to Queeney:

> Is it not terrible that I should now be ashamed to be the friend of one in whose friendship I so lately gloried? My dearest Queeney, how can we help your mother to regain her happiness without recourse to this most unfortunate liaison?

Liaison, indeed! How dared they, how dared they?

Here is a copy of a letter Mrs Montague wrote to Mrs Vesey.

Mrs Thrale's possible marriage has taken such horrible possession of my mind, that I cannot revert to any other subject.
I am sorry and feel the worst kind of sorrow, that which is
blended with shame. I am myself convinced that the poor
woman is mad and indeed have long suspected her mind
was disordered. She was the best mother, the best wife, the
best friend, the most amiable member of society. She gave
the most prudent attention to her husband's business during
his illness and death. What has become of her? I bring in the
verdict – lunacy.

I can tell you, I found all this very hard to withstand.
Tittle-tattle in the newspapers – it's all very well to read
it about other people, but about oneself – it's unbearable!
And then there were my daughters scolding and fussing
away. Poor Piozzi did not know where he stood. I rapidly
became ill and he was distressed to be the cause of it. The
newspapers were not long before they started on him too.
There was a preposterous story that Piozzi was my half-
brother, my father's own son by an Italian mother, and
all because I mentioned once that in looks he was as
handsome as the Salusburys. And as to the allusions to
Italian male sopranos – they were enough to drive him
away from England for ever. It all became too much for
me to bear. To give him up seemed the only thing left.
I made an appointment with Piozzi – such an ordeal, I
had to take an emetic beforehand. I told him of my
decision to sacrifice our happiness.

He went home to Wigmore St. He collected all my
letters, promises of marriage etc. and returned with them,
giving them to Her! 'Take your Mama,' he cried, 'and

make of her a countess! It shall kill me, never mind, but it shall also kill her!'

I wrote in my diary two days later: 'Adieu to all that's dear, to all that's lovely. I am parted from my life, my soul, my Piozzi.'

He returned to Italy. What else could he do? And I came here – to Bath.

I could not bear to be seen in London, for I was ill and looked frightful. I developed erisipelas, a horrid eruption of the skin, and I was so thin I was sure a sharp knife would cut me in two.

Never again have I suffered as I suffered that year. Dr Johnson's words often rang in my head: 'No person, madam, ever yet treated love with contempt except from stupidity ... nature will vindicate her own feelings and revenge the insults offered her.'

I never stopped to enquire how Dr Johnson came by this knowledge. Did he perhaps suffer on my account as I suffered on Piozzi's? I am ashamed to say that I was too selfish, too wrapped up in my own misery even to consider the matter. Johnson was ill too at this time and wrote me several letters, which I ignored. He wrote me one that I can never think of without regret:

I have loved you with virtuous affection. I have honoured you with sincere esteem. Let not all our endearments be forgotten, but let me have in this great distress your pity and your prayers. You see I yet turn to you with my complaints as to a settled and unalienable friend. Do not, do not drive me from you for I have not deserved either neglect or hatred.

The poor doctor did not understand that I too was ill, that the depression I had fallen into had taken away my energies. My daughters eventually came to realise that I was really ill and Queeney condescended to come and see me. The younger girls were all at school. I remember very well her first words to me.

'You are looking frightful, Mama. You are so thin and your skin is revolting. Are you not eating?'

I replied quite insincerely that I was all the better for her coming to see me. We both knew the reason for her visit, but for a time we avoided it.

'You have heard of Dr Johnson's stroke?' said Queeney grimly.

'Yes,' I replied, 'but he is recovering well enough. He has written to me.'

'He misses your care nevertheless.' I could bear it no longer.

'All of you wish me to marry him, that I know. But I have been one man's nurse; I do not wish to be another's. Dr Johnson is thirty years my senior. He has been my confidant, my father, my friend – but husband, never. Queeney, concealed fire burns very fatally. Concealed thoughts lead to wickedness and madness. If you want me to live, you must let me have my way in this. I will send for Piozzi. Sam Johnson once said to me on another matter – "whatever you do, do it but ponder no more." I must do it now, Queeney. I must send for him or die.'

The next day, after an interview with my doctor, she grudgingly consented to put no further obstacles in my way. With trembling hands, I addressed letters to Italy.

A long period would have to elapse before my lover could return. Pray God he still wanted to come.

> My diary, second July, 1784. The happiest day of my whole life, I think. Yes, quite the happiest. My Piozzi came home yesterday and dined with me. My spirits were too much agitated, my heart too much dilated, I was too painfully happy then. My sensations are more quiet today and my felicity less tumultuous. I have spent the night as I ought, in prayer and thanksgiving. May the Almighty preserve my blessings. 'Tis all over now.

We were married at St James's Church, Bath, on 25th July 1784. Soon I was to set off for the finest country in the world with the most excellent man in it. Only my daughters clouded my happiness and my parting with Her was a chilly one. But good-bye to all that. A new country awaited me, a new love and new experiences.

Excuse me. I must get up and move about a little. I shall dance a little, practise my steps for my assembly. At my age, one soon grows stiff with sitting. Dancing has always been one of my favourite forms of exercise. Dancing and horse-riding and bathing. Mr Thrale did not approve of my riding but then while I was his wife, I was nearly always pregnant, so perhaps it is not surprising. When Piozzi and I bought our estate in Wales, I used to bathe in the stream at the bottom of the garden. So stimulating. Two footmen used to convey me down the garden in a sedan chair. They did not watch me bathe, of course.

People are always intrigued as to why I fell so much in love with Piozzi. Well, at my age, they probably think I have forgotten. But I have not forgotten. It is a fallacy of the young to imagine that the old no longer feel emotion. We only pretend not to, that's all.

For the first time I had met a person who cared for me as a person in my own right. To Piozzi, I was not the future mother of his children or the hostess at his dinner-table. I was his companion, his friend. True, I was also that to Dr Johnson, but for me the spark of romance was never added in that direction. Of course, my enemies said that Piozzi married me for my money. But he knew he did not and I knew he did not, so let our enemies say what they please.

We were away from England for three years following our marriage. Exile following a scandal – of course not! Travelling was a tedious business in our day, the roads generally bad and the inns not always clean. But Piozzi and I were happy enough in our honeymoon coach. He had a special little travelling piano and he would play and sing to me. Then we told each other jokes, our favourites being puns, like...

'A gentleman had a spot of grease on his coat! I am got into Greece, cried he. Methinks, said a wag, you go a long way for your pun. On the contrary, cried he, I make it on the spot.'

Here is another:

'A lady had become very ill. Her foot had mortified and dropped off. She looked very ill, but how could she look any better, cried a wag, when she had one foot in the grave!'

Stupid, I know. But when one is happy and in love, one is often stupid.

The main purpose of our journey was to visit Italy together and for me to visit my husband's family. This we did in Venice. They were very cordial towards us, but a little less so, I think, when my husband refused to allow any discussion of my fortune or possible ways of investing it for the benefit of his brothers.

The cities of Italy were each different. In Milan, we had a splendid house, complete with coaches and servants for only eighty pounds a year. In Venice we floated in a gondola – well, who does not? In Rome, I was very disappointed. The wretchedness and dirt were disgusting and spoiled one's enjoymennt of the buildings. In Florence, we enjoyed the company of a group of very convivial English, but in Lucca we were driven away by gnats, scorpions and spiders. Vesuvius was erupting when we arrived in Naples and we managed to get a room with a splendid view.

Why am I talking about Italy? I have not thought about Italy for years. Oh yes, this young man, this young man from the *Bath Gazette*. I don't suppose he will want to hear about Italy, in any case. Queeney scarcely wrote to me while we were away. On my part, I wrote most conscientiously. Many people said I should not have left my children, but my children did not care whether I left them or not.

On our return from Italy in March 1787, I wrote this in my diary:

We have taken a house in Hanover Square for the remainder of the season. London is larger and more lovely than ever. The increasing population, riches and splendour are scarcely credible. Its superiority to all other capital cities is very striking. For our first assembly, we had nearly a hundred people in our rooms. We are going to be all the fashion again, and Piozzi seems happier here than I ever expected to see him. The Miss Thrales, alas, are standoffish still, but in time they may come round.

Sam Johnson had died while we were in Italy. The press were very unkind to me at the time, but nevertheless they were only too anxious to see whether I would publish my memoirs of the doctor. There were many contenders to write his life, and Mr Boswell was in the end the most successful. Personally, I have to admit that I never liked the man and you can learn from his writings what he thought of me.

In the end, I published some stories and recollections and my first little book ran into four editions. Queeney, of course, reported that the blue-stockings were antagonistic, but *The London Chronicle* stated that I had given a true picture of the real Johnson. The *Gentleman's Magazine* wrote, 'the foregoing anecdotes are evidently the production of a vigorous and cultivated understanding. The style in some parts bears the marks of haste but the general execution is worthy of a writer whose powers are held in the highest estimation.'

I was sufficiently encouraged to follow this with the publication of Dr Johnson's letters to me. I wrote to Queeney on the subject. I have a copy here:

> You have perhaps heard from others what I ought to tell you first. My letters written by Dr Johnson are loudly claimed by the public and I shall print 'em directly. What shall I do with the dear name of Queeney? Scratch it out and put in Miss Thrale, I suppose? It occurs very often but always mentioned with tenderness and respect. Tell me what you would have me do and assure yourself that nothing is more precious to me than your approbation.

Queeney's reply was chilliness itself:

> Do what you like with your letters, mama, and print what you see fit. I myself declare that my own testimonies of confidence from dear Dr Johnson shall never see the light. But my sense of delicacy is perhaps superior to that of the wife of an Italian singing master.

What impudence! I was careful never to show this letter to Piozzi.

My letters came out a year after we returned to London. They sold two thousand copies immediately. The dear *Gentleman's Magazine* was once more my champion:

> We cannot see there is anything unjustifiable in this publication, [they wrote]. We think Dr Johnson would have said, Sir, what harm is there in the business? Do the letters deduct from the man's good fame? Do they prove him less a gentleman or more a fool? He has written to a woman as a man writes when he writes to a woman and to children as a wise man writes to children. Sir, a laurel has its small branches as well as its big ones. Sir, when you come to be a great man, you will know that such trifles as these go to make up a great man's fame.

I love the press when they write so. It is pleasant to see one's work so praised.

There I was at forty-seven, a literary celebrity at last. Sometimes, I thought of Mr Marriot: 'Ah, Miss Salusbury, you will be the great poetess of our age.' I was not, of course. My fame rested on Dr Johnson. All my adult life, in some ways I have lived in his shadow. Well, it was a large enough shadow in all conscience and I have enjoyed a large renown. All that was thirty years ago and here are the papers, the diaries, which bring it all back. It has been a very long decline, like growing old, so slow you hardly notice it. My life with Piozzi was in many ways the happiest time of all and yet it was a decline. We grew tired of London after a while. I began to have a longing for the haunts of my childhood and I took Piozzi to Wales.

It would have been a great grief to me if he had failed to share my love of the country of my birth. My journey there with Henry Thrale and the doctor had been near to a disaster. They neither of them expected much of Wales and were not disappointed. Whenever we encountered a really striking prospect, Dr Johnson insisted on confining his eyes to the pages of a book. I found it most annoying. Queeney was twelve at the time and we were unwise enough to allow her to accompany us. Of course, she was a great trial in the coach. The doctor hit on the device of giving her a groat for every goat she counted but soon regretted it, for there were goats in profusion!

But there was no such trouble with Piozzi. He declared that the Vale of Clwyd was like his own dear plain of Lombardy. In time we settled there and built a beautiful house. Brynbella, we called it. I fear I shall never see it again. Here is the poem I wrote for our twentieth wedding anniversary. We were very lucky – we had more than twenty years of happiness:

> Accept, my love, this honest lay
> Upon our twentieth wedding day.
> I little hoped that life would stay
> To hail the twentieth wedding day.
> If you've grown gouty, I've grown gray
> Upon our twentieth wedding day.
> Perhaps there's few feel less decay
> Upon a twentieth wedding day:
> And many of those who used to pay
> Their court upon our wedding day
> Have melted off, and died away
> Before the twentieth wedding day.
> What mercy 'tis we are spared to say
> We have seen our twentieth wedding day.

By then, my poor Piozzi suffered terribly from the gout. It is a secret I have kept long to myself, but he was over-fond of wine. We had a fine cellar at Brynbella and Piozzi had a little sitting-room close to the cellar door, so that servants could bring bottles for him to taste the vintages. Not that he spent all his days drinking. He was very proud of our beautiful estate and concerned himself with the poor of the parish and also with repairs to the church. Here is a note in my diary for our wedding anniversary, July 25th 1800: 'Piozzi has contrived a feast for thirty-five poor haymakers to celebrate our wedding day.'

The winter of that year was dreadful. In parts of Wales, they unthatched their cottages to fodder their cattle. Times are better now. I have never seen such poverty in Bath as I have seen in Wales.

I do not care to remember Piozzi's death. His gout at length turned to gangrene. I never smell incense in church without remembering how it was burnt at Brynbella to hide the smell of his poor, putrid flesh. Of all the deaths of loved ones which I have endured, his was the most terrible. Was it a punishment from God? But why should He punish us for the enjoyment of a quiet and virtuous happiness? My dear Dr Johnson believed most fervently in Hell. Well, Piozzi suffered his Hell here on earth. No God could make him suffer further. He died in the spring of 1809. I wrote in my diary:

> All is over and my second husband's death is the last thing recorded in my first husband's present. Cruel death! Twenty years passed in Piozzi's enchanting society seemed like a happy dream of twenty hours.

For once in her life, on this occasion, She was kind. I wrote to her:

> You have written very kindly. So have all my girls. All very good and very amiable. I have less right to my little hoard of sorrow than I wish for in my ppresent state of mind. But to part, as I did yesterday, for ever from the man who has engrossed my heart for so long a course of years must cost a cruel pang. You know it must.

I was sixty-eight. That is no age at all, you know, for a

woman in good health and with determination. And with some money, of course. Piozzi had been a very prudent husband and I have not been ill provided-for. I have continued writing since Piozzi's death; I began a new diary and other projects not yet published.

The guest list for my eightieth birthday assembly will be published in the *Bath Gazette* on Wednesday. Sir John Salusbury of Brynbella will be at the head. He is Piozzi's brother's child and my heir. His knighthood cost me five thousand pounds. The girls thoroughly dislike him. The guest list – there are so many names I would like to add.

My dear father ... 'My heart aches when I write to thee. When and where will this letter find thee. Please God we shall meet, never to part again.'

My charming Mr Marriot: 'Oh, Miss Salusbury, you are poetry itself. Please recite some stanzas of your own.'

Should I like Henry Thrale to come to my assembly, I wonder? No doubt he would criticise the supper and sleep through the concert. But he was a handsome man. I should not mind dancing with him once more.

Ah, but there is no company now to rival Mr Burke and little Dr Goldsmith and my dear doctor. 'Could she but hold that tongue of hers, could she but restrain that little whirligig, she would be the first woman ...'; nay, but I was the first woman for you, doctor. I was the first woman, the only woman. How we laughed together, what stupid anedotes we recorded.

There were two odd-looking tall young ladies about the town, who were constantly in every public place. Colonel

H. L. Piozzi (Mrs. Thrale) 1793 by G. Dance
National Portrait Gallery, London

Gabriel Piozzi 1793 by G. Dance
National Portrait Gallery, London

Joshua Reynolds (1723-1792)
Mrs. Thrale and her Daughter Hester (Queeney), 1781
Oil on canvas 58½″×55¼″
Gift of Lord Beaverbrook, Beaverbrook Art
Gallery, Fredericton, New Brunswick, Canada

Samuel Johnson 1756 by Joshua Reynolds
National Portrait Gallery, London

Boden dines with us and there were boiled rabbits with the jaws set up like ears. 'What have we here,' said the Colonel, 'our friends the two Miss Gells?'

The resemblance struck everyone and the laughter was loud.

A Miss Murphy dined with us one day. We were making toasts together and Miss Murphy was asked for hers. She said naively, 'What we talk on least and think on most.' There was a roar of laughter from the men and Miss Murphy wondered what was the matter.

The size of a man's understanding can always be known by his mirth. So said my doctor. Oh, were I to produce a score of his sayings as proof of his wit, it would be like showing a handful of pearls to evince the riches of the great Mogul.

But all the time we had together, all the fame which derived from his friendship, I would give them up gladly to have my Piozzi again . . .

I am growing sleepy. Dropping off in my chair like an old woman.

Of course, I am in Bath. For the moment, I imagined myself back in Brynbella. Queeney must bring me some more tea to wake me up. I have not nearly done sorting my papers.

Once the assembly is over and she is gone, I shall be very comfortable, just with my maid again.

'Queeney, some more tea if you please.'

POSTSCRIPT

Mrs Thrale died on 2 May 1821, just over three months after her eightieth birthday.

At her party, she had danced with 'astonishing elasticity' until early in the morning. The expense, however, did leave her temporarily in debt and she let her house, Number 8 Gay Street in Bath, and went to cheap lodgings in Clifton. It was at Clifton that she died, from a chill following a fall.

She was buried, with her dear Piozzi, in the family vault at Tremeirchion Church, not far from Brynbella.

In 1909, the following inscription was placed in the church:

> Near this place are interred the remains of Hester Lynch Piozzi, Dr Johnson's Mrs Thrale. Witty, vivacious and charming, in an age of genius, she ever held a foremost place.

A long list of her writings is preserved in the British Museum, which also contains the printed editions of Gabriel Piozzi's music.

POEMS WRITTEN BY
MRS THRALE AND DR JOHNSON

To Hester Thrale on her Thirty-Fifth Birthday from Sam Johnson

Oft in danger, yet alive,
We are come to thirty-five.
Oft may better years arrive,
Better years than thirty-five.

Could philosophers contrive
Life to stop at thirty-five.
High to soar and deep to dive,
Nature gives at thirty-five.

Ladies, stock and tend your Live,
Trifle not at thirty-five!
For however we boast and strive,
Life declines from thirty-five;
And those who wisely wish to wive
Must look on Thrale at thirty-five.

🎵 Dr Johnson's Mrs Thrale 🐿

An Italian song adapted by Dr Johnson in praise of Mrs Thrale

Viva, viva, la Padrona!
Tutta bella e tutta buona,
La Padrona un Angiolella,
Tutta buona et tutta bella,
Tutta bella et tutta buona
Viva, viva la Padrona!

Long may live my lovely Hetty,
Always young and always pretty,
Always pretty, always young,
Live my lovely Hetty long.
Always young and always pretty,
Long may live my lovely Hetty!

Lines written by Mrs Thrale as a Young Bride

(A period in her life when she was very lonely)

To a Robin Redbreast

Gentle bird a moment stay,
Nor so soon amid the throng,
Of feathered folks the woods among,
Sweetly sing or wildly stray,
Gentle bird a moment stay
Harmoniously a while to cheer
The sorrows of the drooping year.

Do thou to every conscious gale
That breathes on Streatham's verdant vale,
Of nuptial bliss record the sweets
And sing of Streatham's calm retreats;
Her long drawn walk, her piny grove,
Where happiness has deigned to rove.

Where love and peace and friendship join
A wreath for Hymen's brows to twine,
Where you like me have most delight to prove
The joys of rural life and sweet connubial love.

*Lines written by Hester Thrale for a portrait of Henry
Thrale by Sir Joshua Reynolds*

See Thrale from intruders defending his door,
While he wishes his house should with people run o'er
Unlike his companions, the make of his mind
In great thing expanded, in small things confin'd,
Yet his purse at their call, his meat to their taste,
The Wits he delighted in lov'd him at last.
And finding no prominent folly to sneer at,
Respected his wealth and applauded his merit.
Much like that empirical chemist was he,
Who thought Anima Mundi the great Panacee.
Yet when every kind element hep'd his collection
Expir'd while the Med'cine was yet in Projection.

Translation by Mrs Thrale of a love song by Gabriel Piozzi

> For love – I can't abide it,
> The treacherous rogue I know;
> Distrust – I never tried it
> Whether t'would sting or no:
>
> For Flavia many Sighs are
> Sent up by sad Despair:
> And yet poor simple I, Sir,
> Am hasting to the Snare.

Lines written by Mrs Thrale, welcoming Piozzi back to
England, 1784

Over mountains, rivers, vallies, see my love returns to
    Calais.
After all their taunts and malice, entering safe the gates of
    Calais.
While delayed by winds he dallies, fretting to be kept at
    Calais,
Muse, prepare some sprightly sallies to divert my dear at
    Calais,
Say how every rogue that rallies envies him who waits at
    Calais,
For her that would disdain a palace – compared to Piozzi
    – love – and Calais.